# BEYOND
# COMMON THOUGHT

# BEYOND COMMON THOUGHT

---

## THE JOY OF BEING YOU

---

Jacqueline T. Snyder

---

**WINDSOR HOUSE PUBLISHERS**

First edition ©April, 1990 (Hardcover Limited Edition)
Second edition ©July, 1990 (First softcover trade edition)

WINDSOR HOUSE PUBLISHERS
1420 NW Gilman Blvd., Suite 2152, Issaquah, Washington 98027

Library of Congress Cataloging-in-Publication Data

Snyder, Jacqueline T.
        Beyond Common Thought: the joy of being you

        ISBN 0-9625812-0-8

*This book is dedicated
to that which since childhood has
held me in fascination and delight,
and today continually holds me
breathless, exhilarated, quietly moved
—as well as deeply grateful to be a part of
. . . Life
. . . Glorious Life
in all its many forms and dazzling expressions.*

*I dedicate this book
. . . to Life
. . to God.*

# Acknowledgements

I STARTED THIS BOOK sitting near the warmth of my fireplace, pencil in hand, as I marveled at the brilliant turning colors of maple leaves outside my window in the crisp fall air. The work on the book continued through the first and last quiet snowfall upon the land, which then gave way to flower bulbs peaking, inching upward to announce the coming of a dazzling new spring. I would follow the early morning summer sun as its lazy warm rays shone through my windows. . . . Still with pencil in hand and stacks of paper mounting in proportion with my satisfaction, the book evolved all the way through to the next winter's snow. Consistently and always supportive were my family . . . and my editor. . . .

I acknowledge my husband Eddie for his ability to be all he is and his ever-evolving awareness, which includes the supporting and nurturing of me. Sometimes this was natural for him and at other times it was learned and developed, contributing to creating the space I need to be me . . . and all my selves. I acknowledge two very special people, my sons Séan and Brandon. The love and pride I feel for them is well placed, and I acknowledge their ability to follow so well their father's lead of never complaining of my time and devotion to this book. . . .

From season to season and page to page, from fatigue to fulfillment, I am again especially fortunate with my dedicated editor, Scott Miners, whose efforts and presence remain throughout these pages.

My sincere thanks to my copy editor, George Fowler, for his excellence and a polishing touch so appreciated and honored. He especially, as well as myself and Scott, brings a lifelong dedication and devotion to the message reflected within the pages of this book.

I also wish to acknowledge, in addition to his personal efforts, my friend and associate Norman Ratner for his equally loving support and enthusiasm, as well as my friend and secretary Martha Prince, my sister Sandra Best, my dear friend and mother-in-law Juanita Kerns, and my many friends whose presence, encouragement and enthusiasm I deeply value. Among them are Bill Howden, Candi Conradi, Sheila Kenny, Marilyn Fletcher, Sunny and Stanley Swartz, Heather Burch, Dick Davies and all of my supportive friends in San Diego and Florida and many more across the country, whose identity I trust they themselves well know.

I also acknowledge for their unique blend of intelligence and wisdom, the fine man who is my father, Elwood William Tweet, Sr., my mother, Elta Mae Duncan Tweet and my brothers and sisters.

I salute all the "teachers" who have graced my life.

From the depth of my being I acknowledge for their love and support and essence "Sweet Pea" Adelle Tinning, and, on the highest of frequency and whose value and profoundness in my life is beyond all measure . . . my beloved "Z."

—J.T.S.

# Contents

*Whenever you go out of doors, draw the chin in, carry the crown of the head high, and fill the lungs to the utmost; drink in the sunshine; greet your friends with a smile, and put soul into every hand-clasp.*

*Do not fear being misunderstood; and never waste a minute thinking about your enemies. Try to fix firmly in your mind what you would like to do, and then without violence of direction you will move straight to the goal.*

*Keep your mind on the great and splendid things you would like to do; and then, as the days go gliding by, you will find yourself unconsciously seizing upon the opportunities that are required for the fulfillment of your desire, just as the coral insect takes from the running tide the elements it needs. Picture in your mind the able, earnest, useful person you desire to be, and the thought you hold is hourly transforming you into that particular individual.*

*Thought is supreme. Preserve a right mental attitude—the attitude of courage, frankness and good cheer. To think ... is to create. All things come through desire, and every sincere prayer is answered. We become like that on which our hearts are fixed.*

*Carry your chin in and the crown of your head high. We are gods in the chrysalis.*

*—Fra Elbertus*

Humans evolved, cultures advanced,
knowledge accumulated . . .
and all the while, because humans
were also divine,
the whole of the world,
the mind of God,
moved with them

*Humanity has every reason to place the proclaimers of high moral standard and values above the discoverers of objective truth. What humanity owes to personalities like Buddha, Moses, and Jesus ranks for me higher than all the achievements of the enquiring and constructive mind.*
—Albert Einstein, The Human Side

# Preface

THE PROPHETS AND HOLY ONES OF ALL CULTURES and religions ultimately meet in spirit with their words and deeds in a temple of pure truth.

Is there not but one obscured message in the worldwide faiths and belief systems expressed through the veils of culture, languages, metaphors and storyforms, written and oral. Is, indeed, humanity one with that Divinity variously called Absolute, God, Creator, Source, Brahman, the Great Spirit, Allah, Sunyata, World Mother/Father Principle?

Where else can the message of Moses, Jesus of Nazareth, Gautama Buddha, Zarathustra (Zoroaster), Mohammed, Socrates and all the saints and sages meet in common agreement, save in the temple within the mind and heart of humankind?

Wholly equal with these prophets is each human who desires to feel and live his or her own Divinity. The messengers may vary, but the message is similar: "Know and love yourself, and through that experience all things will be revealed to you."

Let us take a look at how it is we are here in what has been called "the human condition." One of the myths[1] of the human race proclaimed that the human spirit, a spark of the Divine, journeyed to life on Earth, its terrestrial adventure, and therein it merged with the material world. Here it forgot its own Divinity because it was shrouded in the veil of matter. Humans became self-perceived orphans, apparently separated from the parent spirit of God.[2]

The story continued that eventually one and then another became tired of a sense of emptiness, a void within, a feeling of separation from what was called God. These few, through their desire to experience this God, finally remembered that the self is always divine even in matter, even in human form. They realized therefore the bounty of self. They shared their realizations with their

---

[1] Myth: a story pointing to a truth that cannot be told in words alone. One must at times go beyond words in order to embrace an expanded meaning.

[2] The term *God* used throughout this book is used to refer to the Eternal, Ultimate Source, without meaning to restrict the term to its usual usage.

---

# Introduction

LET'S LOOK BACK AT HISTORY, at a few of those who created inspired works of art or literature. I speak of works that live in seeming perpetuity because of their universality. It is fascinating to find these creations of the human mind that bear the mark of greatness seem to come from a state of consciousness beyond the ordinary.

Mozart spoke of his personal inspiration in accessing expanded realms of consciousness. At the end of the 18th Century, in personal correspondence he wrote to a friend:

> When I am, as it were, completely myself, entirely alone and of good cheer, say, traveling in a carriage or walking after a good meal, or during the night when I cannot sleep, it is on such occasions that my ideas flow best and most abundantly. Whence and how they come I know not, nor can I force them. Those

pleasures that please me I retain in memory, and am accustomed, as I have been told, to hum them to myself. If I continue in this way it soon occurs to me how I may turn this or that morsel to account so as to make a good dish of it, that is to say, agreeable to the rules of counterpoint, to the peculiarities of the various instruments. All this fires my soul, and, provided I am not disturbed, my subject enlarges itself, becomes methodized and defined, and, on the whole, though it would be long, stands almost complete and finished in my mind so I can survey it, like a fine picture or a beautiful statue at a glance. Nor do I hear in my imagination the parts successively, but I hear them, as it were, all at once.[1]

Picasso said, "While I work, I leave my body outside the door the way Moslems take off their shoes before entering the Mosque." In their autobiographies many creative people, scientists, authors, artists, inventors describe unique moments of breakthrough to creativity, to inspiration.

Who knows how many scholars and thinkers were similarly inspired. . . . Perhaps some of them knew and held the secret within themselves; their source had an identity, even a name. Perhaps not. Some in their discretion let their creation be accepted as it was at the time, at face value, without touting the fact that a mystical source had inspired them—as with Charles Dickens, as with Mohammed and his Angel.

---

[1]In P.E. Vernon, Ed. *Creativity: Selected Readings* (Penguin, 1970)

I have found myself, as have many others, in a similar category with Dickens, Mozart and Mohammed. I have had times of inspiration as Mozart did when I could not ascribe it to any voice, and I have also at other times seen music, felt wisdom and heard a divine voice.

I feel that it will be a stretch for some people to understand what I am now going to say.

For those people who may feel all of their spiritual knowledge must come only from a pulpit, in a grand cathedral or synagogue, it is a stretch. For some who want to read their spiritual wisdom and feel it is credible only if from an ancient manuscript, a strong religious lineage handed down from antiquity, or if found in a buried jar in a desert and verified by scholars—what I am saying here will also be a stretch. This is also true for anyone who feels spiritual knowledge must come from dimly lit rooms by spiritual mediumship, believing it is more pure and direct from God if without the influence of human touch.

I fall in none of these categories and in all of them; that is, in a sense, I accept them all and reject them all. I accept the thread of truth that runs through all that speaks of an unseen consciousness and intelligence that is divine and available, whether accessed by an inspired minister, artist, disciple, devotee, musician, writer or prophet in their pure desire to know.

What I reject is all of the interpretation and limiting dogma and beliefs that inhibit and distance people from the simple thread of truth that exists in all traditions. I further reject whatever inhibits anyone from their own creative Divinity and the simplicity of God-understanding. I transcend whatever distances people from understanding that this is innately within all of us now and not something to be attained in the future.

This message may be a stretch for some people. However, spiritual wisdom is timeless and is increasingly evident in these modern times, everywhere and with many people and many situations in life.

Whether it comes from script writers in the motion picture industry as a contemporary "Field of Dreams" or as Luke Skywalker who hears the voice of a deceased Obi-Wan-Kenobi advise him, "Close your eyes Luke, and feel your way"—it is all wisdom that points to an unseen reality. It can include a Shirley MacLaine who has a spiritual experience on a mountaintop in Peru and the courage to write about it. It can manifest in a medical doctor named Bernie Siegel, who in meditation listens to the voice of a guide and brings to modern medicine revolutionary ways of healing. But are they revolutionary, or are they ancient? Some have referred to Siegel as a medical prophet. How appropriate!

Not all prophets need to have lived in antiquity. Other researchers, such as Elizabeth Kubler-Ross, M.D., psychologist Ken Ring and Raymond Moody, M.D., have compiled thousands of files on those who have had a death experience and "returned" to tell of a glorious light, a loving voice, a light being or a religious figure they have met. What is it about films, such as "Always" or "It's a Wonderful Life" and "Oh God" and the story of Scrooge, who travels with a guiding spirit through the times of Christmas past, present and future? These all point to the influence of the unseen world of consciousness and through the media of literature, film and stage capture the imagination of the masses of people.

For many it is a stretch to bring this world to daily life and common thought. But for me it is a part of everyday life.

This book is for all of the people who exist on our planet who want more . . . who through greater understanding want to reengage their enthusiasm for life and reverse some of the anesthesia they may have created in order to cope . . . . In the tapestry of life is a thread of timeless truth and simplicity: *we exist in a supportive sea of consciousness that some call God.*

For those who wonder who I am, I reply simply that I am just what we all are. We are all, in a sense, transmitters, receivers of thought. Our intent and will and desire and focus have everything to do with what we can access and then express from that experience. My intent is to celebrate life, to accentuate it, its purpose and its meaning, to reveal and explore its mystique.

The message in this book must speak for itself: its origin, its divinity, its intent of love and peace and its support of humankind and life. As I write this Introduction after the book is completed, I find I have gained greater wisdom and meaning concerning its content. I have found that nothing truly stands alone. Whether it is a discovery in medicine, of science or an inspired book, whether a man or woman reaches great heights and becomes an inspiration to the world, such an event never happens alone!

Having already acknowledged that this book is inspired from higher realms, I must also speak of my own thread of wisdom in it, what I know and live in my life, what I have tested and applied. There is as well the thread of those whom I have quoted and who give it balance from their research and given expertise. Too, there are the contributions of many friends and family members whose life experiences also bring their threads to weave into this tapestry of wisdom.

Often as I look down from an airplane window over the lights of a metropolitan city or the sprawling farmlands and the meandering ribbons of highways and country roads, time seems to suspend itself, and I recall a young child riding in the family car who looked out at distant city lights and wondered at the "how" of it all. Now, as an adult, as I peer out the windows of an airplane continually in awe at the splendor of life, I contemplate the fragileness of all the people who have yet to know of the common miracle in which they participate.

I have realized that if God, as looked upon by so many as an unseen entity separate from humankind, could create the peace on Earth that is desired, the prosperity and wellness among humanity, with love among people, surely it would have been done by now. In acknowledgement of the free will of which we are endowed, therefore, it seems it is only *we* who can bring this about. This being the desire of our times, may this book be of assistance on how to live this desired understanding.

Through the passing of time we have been influenced by religions, mythologies, saints, sages and their grand writings. These have prepared many of us so that today we find ourselves to have grown much in understanding. Respectfully honoring all teachings, I believe the world is now at the threshold of a race-wide advancement in that awareness possessed for centuries by a few. There is a exponentially growing consciousness today that God is the Source that is expressed individually and uniquely through each and every person. This is more and more confirmed for me by my personal and public interviews with leaders in their given fields of science, theology, medicine and psychology.

There are certainly great men and women, in the churches, synagogues, cathedrals and monasteries of God, yet it is also when people of day-to-day life who not just understand, but learn how to live this understanding that it ceases to be a philosophy only. That is when it gains a more prominent place in the life of humankind—in the marketplace, in the home, in the seats of power—everywhere. Only in this way will the balance needed for the peace we desire come into our world.

As long as we think we can love a God and honor a God who sits upon a cloud in a place called heaven, and yet can judge and harm one another in the name of this God, we do not support peace in our world!  When we learn to see the Divine within, then we can also see it in one another, and then indeed we can more easily love and allow in the name of God—and thereby assist society to become one that honors the individual expression of that God within each of its members.

For many people, what I am about to say concerning God is controversial or provocative. For others it is simply an understanding. Either way, I feel it is an important perspective for our world and for our times.

Therefore I offer this book with the words of Emerson in *On God and Man:*

> Happy is he who looks only unto his work to know if it will succeed, never to the times or public opinion; and who writes from the love of his heart certain thoughts and not for the necessity of sale—who writes always to the *unknown friend.*

—J. T. S.

Editor's Note:
Like the continual discovery of hidden treasures in the rereading of timeless poetry, we suggest also that a quiet rereading of many of these chapters will reveal new understandings as they seemingly emerge in the text through the gained insights of you the reader.

Beliefs are the doorways through which
everything we want must pass

*You are a distinct portion of the essence of God; and contain part of God in yourself. Why, then, are you ignorant of your noble birth? Why do you not consider whence you came? Why do you not remember when you are eating, who you are who eat; and whom you feed? Do you not know that it is the Divine you feed; the Divine you exercise? You carry a God about with you.*
*—Epictetus, A.D. 50*

## Chapter One

# The Search for the Divine and the Discovery Within

*Notes in a jar and the diversity of life / doorways of belief / spiritual quest.*

THERE ARE SO MANY DIMENSIONS to the human experience. Life, when reflected upon, reveals a variety of realities that we experience in our collective living adventure. For instance, imagine that on a given day a businessman living on the Atlantic coast is having a fine time in his life. He works on Wall Street and the market is up. On this given day he observes that "Life is wonderful, life is glorious. What I desire comes to me. I feel empowered, and I am happy in my life." He writes this down on a piece of paper and stuffs it into a jar. As time passes the jar is buried in the earth.

On the same day in the midwest of the United States there is a drought, and a farmer has slaved with his hands and yet his farm does not bring forth a crop yield. His heart is burdened, for the food and nourishment for his children is lacking, and his stature and how it appears to his beloved concerns him deeply, for he is the keeper of his family. In a quiet moment alone in the barn he brings forth a pen and paper and writes down, "On this day I am feeling weary and heavy with the responsibility of life. I am burdened with concern for children that I dearly love; yet, nature does not meet my expectations and my crop it is not here. Lonely and isolated I am, for I am a man and I cannot weep to another. It is harsh—life is." And the man puts his notes in a jar which later becomes buried.

On another coast there is a woman who has created an opportunity in her life that is unfolding, and her expectations for life are vast. The energy that runs through her veins throbs with the expectation of a dream that will come to fruition. She has a sense of the vitality of life, and she cherishes it. She looks not to her side here or there, and what matters most to her is the intent she feels. She has a clarity within her soul, and life, it is wondrous! It holds many answers and opportunities and she is filled with purpose. She writes all this on a paper, puts it in a jar and this jar too becomes buried.

Yet, in a very cold and very dark city on a back road there is another who has not a roof over his head. He stands in long lines on windy nights for food. For him hell could be no worse than what he experiences, for his dignity has left him and the anticipation of his youth has been spent on what appears to be dead ends. He writes upon a paper, "I fear not death nor hell, for what could be worse than to lose the sense of pride and distinctiveness of being human—such an existence befalls me." And he puts his paper in a jar that later, as the others did, becomes buried.

All this happens in the same year and on the same day. All are different realities, each being experienced and expressed. Centuries pass and an archaeologist discovers a jar. Depending upon where he digs and what jar he uncovers, he begins to piece together a puzzle, in order to distinguish what life was like for people in that particular year.

Will he get a clear or distorted picture? Neither. He will get an impression of one person's experienced reality. As he reads, he may ask himself, "Is this the truth for all mankind in this year?" He will look for additional pieces of information to tell him more. As he looks he discovers that there are other jars containing descriptions of vastly different life experiences, and all jars were buried at the same time. He contemplates, "How can this be? How is it that God would sit in heaven and allow some to feel such joy and others such remorse?"

# Doorways of Belief

THIS ISSUE of how God could allow such diversity will be addressed in more detail in later chapters where we will explore the role we as humans play in conjunction with the God/Source in creating our own individual and unique reality. It is my understanding that we acquire and develop our beliefs and information through our environment—family, friends, society. This accumulated information filters back and influences our life, and, based on our acquired beliefs, we form and co-create our own reality. India's Mahatma Gandhi had great insight and made a very profound statement about the power of belief when he said, "People often become what they believe themselves to be. If I believe I cannot do something, it makes me incapable of doing it. But when I believe I can, I acquire the ability to do it, even if I didn't have it in the beginning."

What powerful beliefs do you hold? Are they affecting your life positively or negatively? It is a profound realization and it is very important to recognize that *our beliefs are the doorways through which everything we want must pass.*

There is tremendous benefit derived from a review of your life in order to be aware of what beliefs you have. Examine beliefs that may have come from within a limited structure, for you are more than your beliefs, and your identity need not be confined to fit within them. It is also purposeful to know that your physical body may be affected and inhabited by beliefs through mental attitude. There is now much medical and scientific evidence emerging to support that view as can be seen in the field of psychoneuroimmunology. The powers of thought contained within beliefs are life-affecting.

I wish to give you another example in a poignant story about belief told by a speaker from a major corporation. A nightwatchman for a railway yard, upon checking refrigeration cars to make sure no one was taking a free ride, became accidentally trapped inside one of these cars on a cross country train. He knew of the danger and saw no way for himself to get out as the doors locked from outside the car. As the train's journey began the man started to write on the floor of the car, "I see no way out and I am getting colder and colder." He wrote often during the journey about how his energy was slipping away and how, as the cold overtook him more and more, his mind seemed to get less clear. Finally, convinced he was dying, he wrote to those close to him in his life about things he had always wanted to say. When the train stopped and the handlers found the man, he had frozen to death. They were puzzled at reading his long messages on the floor about the cold, for, due to a malfunction, the refrigeration device had never been on.

There are as well, many stories about how patients under hypnosis are so suggestible through the power of their own thoughts that when a hypnotherapist suggests a very hot iron bar is going to be placed on their arms, but in fact a room temperature pencil is used, the patients react with pain anywhere from mild to extreme, and in some cases burn marks even appear. These anecdotal stories point to the power of belief in affecting a person's life.

The point here is that individuals who are unaware of and unattuned to the power of their beliefs are also equally unaware of *their own* profound influence on their lives. They therefore oftentimes perceive themselves to be victims of exterior sources or powers. A certain measure of these experiences will press an individual to ask, "What is going on in my life?" This is often when the exploration of deeper issues begins, and a spiritual quest is undertaken. Many people assume they have not been on such a quest, and that those who are known for their spiritual insights are more advanced because they set out so purposefully on a spiritual journey.

# Spiritual Quest

While I acknowledge that some have an explicitly spiritual goal for their search, perhaps more often than many would realize this quest often originates out of a need to understand the meaning of certain incidents that occur in their personal lives. Those who have begun to explore the deeper meaning of issues confronting them—crises in the world of finance, ecology, parental and other relationships, health and illness—find their examination of these situations often triggers personal change. Ultimately they realize it takes them into greater wisdom and what in hindsight may eventually be termed a "spiritual quest." Even though one sets out to understand a seemingly common question, the quest can lead to understanding in "spiritual" realms and the exploration of questions and answers of ultimate value. Here is also where an individual may take the first steps to finding answers to questions about self—and where one first discovers the problem solving mind that is the province of all.

For myself, I have long wondered about the mystery of life. Long ago in childhood, as my memory serves, I cannot remember a time I did not wonder about God, the Source of life and people everywhere. (I use the term *God* a great deal in this text, because it is a term commonly used when speaking of the mysterious Source of life. I realize there are connotations that come with this term, and there are other terms in different cultures such as *Brahman*, *Atman* and *Allah*, but for simplicity I wish to use the common term *God* to express some uncommon views about the Divine Source. See note 2 in Preface.)

As a child, I wanted to know what my Source was, what life was about and the purpose for which all of us are here. Years passed and I accumulated many interpretations, yet nothing I found felt powerfully enlightening about these subjects. I was exposed to many beliefs, but none seemed to contain the whole answer, and, still perplexed by this mystery, I was usually left frustrated as to what was True, Real and Exact. As time flowed and different people entered and exited my life, I eventually began to put many pieces together.

I believe my curiosity about life helped create the opportunities that came to me to speak with many religious leaders, philosophers, scientists, politicians and celebrities, and everyday people all over the world. All of these experiences contributed to my present view of the God/Source. My view parallels that of the ancient Vedas of India which proclaim, "It is the supreme. . . . It is One without a second. It is the Atman. Know it alone."[1]

Echoes of what I feel are also found in Ralph Waldo Emerson:

Jesus Christ belonged to the true race of prophets. He

---

[1] *Mandukya Upanishad,* 7 Upanishads: The last stage of the Vedic literature, the most ancient scripture known to man, written in Sanskrit and preserved in Indian philosophy. There are one hundred and eight prominent Upanishads. Eleven of them are considered preeminent, where the wisdom of the Veda reaches its acme, the storehouse of philosophical gems. Often referred to as *Vedanta,* or "pinnacle of knowledge" the word *Upanishad* means to "sit close" beside a competent teacher.

saw with open eye the mystery of the soul. Drawn by its severe harmony, ravished with its beauty, he lived in it, and had his being there. ...[H]e estimated the greatness of man....was true to what is in you and me. He saw that God incarnates himself in man, and evermore goes forth anew to take possession of his World. He said, in his jubilee of sublime emotion, "I am Divine. Through me, God acts; through me speaks. Would you see God, see me." [2]

Surely, I have come to feel, as it was with him, so it is with us.

Through my years of exploring I have discovered an overview of many central beliefs that exist in the world. This view has simplified and clarified a great deal for me. I find myself writing the words of this book in an endeavor to share what my life experiences and profound teachers have revealed to me. I am not saying that I alone have found "The Truth" or the only exact answer, but I do feel far more comfortable now understanding God—(supreme thought, consciousness)—as never separate and always present in consciousness for all who seek to know. These thoughts, arriving through the minds of many teachers, have many expressions. As the ancient Greek philosopher

---

[2] *On Man and God*, Ralph Waldo Emerson, Peter Pauper Press, New York, 1961

Heraclitus (500 B.C.) said: "There is only one Wisdom; it is to understand the thought by which all things are steered through all things."

Oftentimes, as I have met people throughout my life who have wanted to express their truth about God and life, I have noticed their inclination to want to fit their beliefs into a box with a bow and give it as a gift: "This is the meaning of life, allow me to pass it on to you. It has come to me from my family and friends and has been passed down through the generations. Open this package. Within it you will discover who God is and how to live your life."

I do not believe Divine Truth can be fit into a package, nor do I believe handing *fixed* truth down as from one pope to the next is necessarily the thing to do. Where in this would be room for the needed evolution of thought and awareness! Beliefs do not necessarily have value simply by being inherited as heirlooms!

We have already been a people warring over such fixed truths for far too many years for that to be the only way. I believe the truth that stands the test of time in the hearts of humanity is one that resonates to all people—all living creatures, plants, animals and all occupants of the universe. It is a truth that transcends creeds, cultures and societies.  It is a truth that weaves us together in a more expansive belief and understanding of who we are, who

God is and how we continually interface with God through one another.

I believe God is a frequency of sublime vibration, enormous intelligence and boundless love—and humanity is the conduit for it. Given our free will and intentionality, we have various adventures which are the expressions of our own attunement to the higher vibration of God.

In my respect for all of you who read this I state my wish for you most clearly: may any wisdom you gain from this message be based wholly on that *which resonates within you* and may you let yourself be guided by that within *you* which desires to know.

The promise of the future is that many
will explore our vast human potential,
and the intuition and creative genius
that will come forth will fuel the
acceleration of our race

*All things by immortal power*
*Near or Far*
*Hiddenly*
*To each other linked are*
*That thou canst not stir a flower*
*Without troubling a star.*
*—Francis Thompson,*
The Mistress of Vision

Chapter Two

# Beyond Common Thought

*The weight of old understandings / expanded
understanding / truth beyond words / contemplation and
insight / illusion of perceived separation from Divine
mind / being all you can be / metaphor of light*

FROM THE BEGINNING OF TIME MANY PEOPLE have related to a supreme being. Regardless of our different regions or religions, we have acknowledged a supreme Source some call "God," "Allah," "Brahman" or "the Divine." In our own and separate ways we have either prayed, chanted, danced or meditated to this Source.

Long has been our search and a quest to know

ourselves. This search has taken us on many wonderful journeys. As has been true for me, I am sure it has also brought many others to wonderful teachers. During this time, however, it is my observation and experience that many have been subject to understandings and words that have led to confusion. A very pervasive example which I find in my talks with others around the country is one in which many people have an experience similar to one that I remember having in childhood. My understanding today is much broader, in that it has expanded to include the teachings of masters from many cultures.

I want to use an example here from my own background in a Christian culture. I had (and still have) a great love and devotion for Jesus of Nazareth. My love then, however, seemed in proportion to my feelings of inadequacy, for I was taught, and I believed the interpretation, that in order to be a Christ one had to be born one. Only later, as I further sought the meaning of Jesus' life, did I expand my understanding of him to embrace the wisdom that he represented an example of *one* who lived in Christ consciousness.

This is the consciousness now being understood at the turn of this century, two thousand years after the life of Jesus. It is now being perceived as the Christ consciousness meant for everyone, as our divine heritage if we so choose.[1]

---

[1] See Chapter 5.

As in this example and various others, numerous interpretations have been heavy on many souls, and grand limitation has been felt as a weight upon the understanding of people in their attempts to comprehend themselves and the universe we all live in.

I would like to begin to examine this confusion by presenting briefly a perspective of how we may have become overly complex in our views of the world, this divine Source and each other. I find a certain truth in T.S. Eliot's quatrain from "Four Quartets":

> We shall not cease from exploration,
> and the end of all our exploring
> will be to arrive where we started
> And know the place for the first time.

The more I observe life, the more I think it has become far more complex than it ever needed to be. A simpler understanding seems necessary to clarify the meaning of life, our purpose here, fulfillment or denial, all of it. In my own experience I have found that, in alignment with my will to know more, a clearer truth can be acquired. This alignment of will also allows a clarity of how it is that we are also as God and yet are at the same time in the physical.

As we advance in desire to personally experience God, and as more seek a peace and joy upon our planet, a new clarity of oneness with one another will be found.

In this vein I wish you to consider with me an uncommon thought: we might be far, far more than many of us have ever suspected we are. With this understanding, as will be elaborated throughout this book, it is reasonable to assume that a commonness with the Source so many call God and with one another shall be desired and therein be revealed. To truly reach the much desired state of co-existence in peace and love on earth that all seem to seek, I feel we must embrace and acknowledge the co-creators we all are, and also recognize God to be expressing physically as man and woman.

# Expanded Understanding

RESPECTFULLY ACKNOWLEDGING THE MANY BELIEFS in the world, I nevertheless would like to suggest a simple exercise here. That is, deep within yourself temporarily, for a brief moment, lay aside all of your present beliefs, no matter how strongly they may grip you, regardless of the emotional, cultural, ancestral or monetary investment you have in them. I am not suggesting that you negate any of your beliefs, for it is important to know that there is purposefulness in all truths that have brought you to who you are in this moment. Nevertheless, if one spends all one's time comparing all that was taught in whatever religion or belief system one was raised in, then how would one be able to go forward into the light of new understanding?

If I take every new concept that comes to me and try to fit it into the understanding that I presently have, then I only conform it to fit into a belief that may not be serving me. We may honor the past teaching of our world and yet respectfully go beyond it, which is exactly what the visionaries have always done.

Visionaries are often those who can hold us spellbound as they weave the tale of futures imagined. They dare to go to the perimeters of present thinking; they journey beyond the realm of conformity and often return to tell others what they have found. Often they inspire nations. They are the pioneers of new thoughts in science, in education, for the future of their race. From the flat to the round earth of Columbus, from the geocentric world to the solar system of Copernicus and from the mechanistic view of Newton to the quantum world of modern physics where consciousness plays a central role in determining reality and where the observer affects the observed, to the modern medical healers such as Bernie Siegel, M.D., who was willing, as so many others, to expand beyond the customary  perimeters of "physician only" and acknowledge the unlimited power of thought and love to heal the body, so often the past has given way to new thought—but for many reluctantly.

As Albert Einstein said, for every new vision of the world there are a thousand self-appointed guardians of the past.

I have learned that it is of grand importance to allow self to simply engage the knowing of the "heart" as well as intellect in order to grow and go beyond words that "guard the past" to their deeper meaning. There may be beliefs many hold that are limited because of the very limits of the words themselves. . . . An entire life then becomes an effect of limited understandings. Imagine, instead, what could happen when the collective people of the human race share the same vision of peace as the visionary leaders of our history.

Visualize all people's inspiration becoming an absoluteness in a world and to a world united for the benefit of all.

# Truth Beyond Words

WHAT IS MEANT BY "GOING BEYOND WORDS" is that thoughts expressed by anyone come originally from the unlimited mind of God; however, thoughts are often conformed to words and other symbols in order to be taught. This is true of all religions, philosophies and belief systems worldwide.

It follows that anything heard or read is always going to be a bit altered and limited; therefore, the *unlimited* understanding desired by many seekers can never be taught in words alone, no matter how exalted the teacher. For anyone to try to limit thought to a word would be to take an understanding that is vast and confine it with a vocabulary that is subject to the interpretation of individuals and cultures. This creates one of many ways in which much of the variedness and distortion of great truths begins. As the words are passed on, shared, they can become highly limited and may potentially start to be controlling of people through individual beliefs about them.

For example, let's reevaluate the interpretations that have been placed upon certain key words in the context of many persons' religious values. The first such word is *sin*. *Sin* literally means "missing the mark," to be off target. More correctly, it means to be out of alignment with God and our purpose of existence in daily life as well as within the cosmos. This personal sense of nonalignment is far more simply corrected and easily overcome than many have made it seem. It is a natural experience, to feel or establish conscious awareness of the God Source within.

This may seem to be an oversimplification, but truly, this felt sense of awareness is only as far away as an open attitude and personal acknowledgement. I wish to stress the word *personal*, for, if alignment with God takes place in personal consciousness, *no one* is needed to "redeem" anyone. There is no redemption from sin by anyone outside oneself, there is only a change in attitude—and it is self-chosen . . . *thus, we are our own redeemers!* It is interesting that one meaning of the word *redeem* is "transformation." It is interesting to note that *transformation* is a more widely used term today, whether in psychology, religion or personal growth.

Another among these misinterpreted words is *repent*,[1] which means "to go beyond limited awareness of self as human only and embrace also the consciousness of God essence," which is an awareness found in the consciousness of a Christ. Scholarly examination has shown that *sin* and *repent* have commonly been misinterpreted respectively as "wrong," and "one must suffer and sacrifice." These terms were often used in such a context that it added to the confusion that there is a singular judgmental and condemning God. Not only did this make it seem more difficult for some to relate to God, but it also clouded terms that simply describe a state of being consciously aligned or attuned. I think our actions today will reveal or

---

[1] Ed. Note: John White, a leading consciousness researcher states: "Over the centuries [the word *repent*] has become misunderstood and mistranslated.... The Aramaic word Jesus used is *tob*, meaning 'to return,' 'to flow back into God.' The sense of this concept comes through best in the Greek word used to translate it. The word is *metanoia* and, like tob, it means something far greater than merely feeling sorry for misbehavior. Metanoia has two etymological roots. Meta means 'to go beyond' or 'to go higher than,' and noia comes from *nous*, meaning 'mind.'. . . [T]he original meaning of metanoia is literally 'going beyond or higher than the ordinary mental state.' In modern terms, it means transcending self-centered ego and becoming God-centered, God-realized." *Quest*, V. 2, No. 2, pp 13-23, 1989

support an emerging understanding in our race that there is no need for using words to control others and keep them within the boundaries of kindness, justness and love toward one another. This type of philosophy shall be replaced with a far more powerful inner code of conduct by which we will harmoniously coexist. This inner code concerning our relationships with one another naturally includes a grace and love toward our fellow man.

I believe every single individual can, like the visionaries, develop the ability that is within each of us to go directly to the Source for the unlimited meaning of any idea, and bypass the limits of any word, which in and of itself was only a symbol of a meaning. *The process of inner reasoning of words to a felt understanding of the truth behind them frees one from their limits.*

# Contemplation and Insight

IF TIME AND AGAIN in contemplation, one would take an understanding and return it to the original thought, or meaning, which is grander than what one has previously heard, then one would become weaned from a need for any particular teacher or religion and would reestablish educated and informed choices.

Meditation and contemplation are terms often associated with enlightened beings, whether the masters associated with certain religions or zen techniques. I feel meditation will be even far more important for day-to-day business people as we near the end of this century. Not only can more coping strategies for stress be found in meditation, but also information for a world where the creative edge is important. Often information in the competitive business world is shared with many, e.g., in trade journals, newsletters, computer data banks, and word of mouth. The competitive edge in the future will not be in shared common data, *but in evoking one's own personal genius.* Through the inspiration and original thought accessed in meditation or contemplation, however, one can excel in new areas of creativity and new ideas that have not been here before. Rarely, I have found, will you find a successful executive, engineer, inventor or any other who has not used this intuitional insight in his or her work. *The promise of the future is that many will explore our vast human potential, and the intuition and creative genius that will come forth will fuel the acceleration of our race.*

As I have observed, the God Source does not seem to distinguish if people go to synagogues, cathedrals, monasteries, to Wall Street, business seminars, think tanks or gurus. What does seem important is that we seek a personal relationship with, and honor and love our Source *within ourselves* as well as in all else. Love of this Source in self, and then all else, is *the foundation of all beneficial personal interaction.* There is not any one right way that is the only way; there must be as many right ways as there are individuals, and each of us needs to honor our own!

This is not to say that we cannot learn or gain from the richness of any tradition, or look for the kernels of truth within each of them that are the common "property" of all. The process of contemplation and meditation, however, carries with it tools of expanded reasoning power that can be brought to daily experience. Many sages have spoken of this ability of the human mind through the use of reason and contemplation to enhance reason and birth an even more knowing part of mind. As the Buddhist sage Tsong-kha-pa noted,[2] "[W]hen given things are analyzed by the most pure discrimination. . . , the faculty of noble insight is born. . . ." He goes on to say that the fire of noble insight expands the more limited aspect of mind so that more insight can be realized. Through thus using reason and deep contemplation in our desire for answers to our questions about life, we can arrive at our own truth and find the courage to live it.

# Illusion of Perceived Separateness from Divine Mind

ONE OF THE CREATION MYTHS orignially explained that a totally separate God reached out into nothingness and

---

[2] Nathan Katz, *Buddhist and Western Philosophy*, 1981, p. 462

created beings from that nothingness. These beings, according to this myth, forever remain separate from God. Some believers eventually developed this myth form and came to believe that this separate God selected some of his creations and made them his adopted children through a mysterious thing called "grace," but even then they remained wholly separate.

A great advance on this story form was made when it was realized that in the act of creation God—or what was by now understood to be Eternal Being—was not creating from nothing *but simply sharing Its own Being* when It "created." Nevertheless, even with this understanding, the notion lingered that we "expressions" of Divine Being were somehow still separate from our Source.

This sense of duality even permeated (and still often permeates) the beliefs of reincarnation. A gap remained, even within this understanding, between us and our God.

Our understanding now needs to evolve to include again our actual and eternal oneness with our God Source. We must come to fully appreciate the fact that it was Its own Self and Being that our Source shared with us when we were expressed ("created") from "It."

I, as well as many others, once assumed that humankind was "lowered" or fallen from the grace of God—that this Source *lowered* Its Light into form. Many feel that because they are "lowered" or "fallen" from the light of "God," they need to go back to this Light. The common phrase is, "I want to 'go' to the light. I want to 'go' home to God. . . ." I believe It is already *within* us in consciousness; therefore, as so many sages of the world have said, we have nothing to acquire, only to realize; we are already there! As Jesus said, "The Kingdom of God is *within* you."

Writing about this divine consciousness, or "mind" that "we are," George Wald, Nobel Laureate and Harvard Professor Emeritus in Biology, eloquently addresses the subject when he says:

[W]hen I speak of mind pervading the universe, of mind as a creative principle perhaps primary to matter, any Hindu will acquiesce, will think, yes, of course, he is speaking of Brahman. The Judeo-Christian-Islamic God *constructed* a universe and just once. Brahman *thinks* a universe and does so in cycles, time without end. As the *Upanishads* tell us, each of us has a share in Brahman, the *Atman*, the essential Self, ageless, imperishable. Tat tvam asi—Thou art That! That is the stuff of the universe, mind-stuff; and yes, each of us shares in it. . . .[3]

---

[3] *Synthesis of Science and Religion: Critical Essays and Dialogues* (Bhaktivedanta Institute, 1986).

# Being All You Can Be

BECAUSE OF SOME OF THE INTERPRETATIONS of creation myths, there has always been a sense of being lowered from God, a separation if you will. From this belief, varied religions, sects and followings have been formed with rules created about how to become divine "again." I firmly believe this very attitude has perpetuated the perceived gap of separation from God, and although *the gap was only an illusion perceived as real*, all life as we know it has been affected by that illusion.

Many people feel unduly minimized by life and yet they could well feel empowered. The most prevalent example of the attitude of so many of feeling separate from their powerful Source in the world is the core feeling of unworthiness. This feeling ripples out and affects relationships and one's sense of abundance. It fosters a feeling of inadequacy and of being dwarfed by life and nature. The mystery or questioned relationship one has with the awesome Source of life seems to pervade, and the attitude is that "I must be infinitesimal compared to all this . . . " instead of feeling empowered by it.

As a result of feeling inadequate, many people develop a "fix-it" attitude. They become susceptible to rules made by people who seemingly "know" how to fix them. Then a consciousness emerges that something is wrong and it needs to be corrected. Therefore we accept rules that one is successful only if one is so tall or so thin or if a certain number of digits are in one's paycheck. Happiness and success then become measured by exterior signs. Soon stress emerges, executives drop out, psycho-emotional complexes arise . . . and it all arises from perceived aloneness.

We need to look for what is already "right" about us, what it is about ourselves innately that we can love and celebrate. In actuality all of life and the Source of life is to empower us, because we are co-creators and are a basic participant in the play of life. Individually, we need to ask, "Who created all this in my personal life?" Perhaps you have something in your life that is there because it originated from a belief, maybe in childhood, that you needed someone's approval. This belief grew stronger within you until you decided you did not have enough within yourself, and you always looked outside yourself for significance. Your core belief was that your value came from outside you. *Value first comes from within*, then you will see the true value of everything else in your world.

There is another pervasive and perhaps more basic example of a core belief that has led to an attitude of lack of worthiness. In our attempts to model ourselves after Jesus of Nazareth, which is an ideal almost the entire Western world and some of the East embraces, many have associated the term *ascension* with becoming all, meaning if we would ascend to God we would have it all—

heaven, peace and so on. At one time in my life, as many of my colleagues did, I held it as an ideal that if I could just be "spiritual" enough, loving enough, I could embrace the ideal held out by Christianity. I have learned that the Christ ideal is one of consciousness; therefore, we *already are* the All . . . .

Christ consciousness consists of the knowledge of this fact, that we are already that which we want to ascend to, and the raising of consciousness is a form of ascension. The more we are in this consciousness of our divine heritage, the more we will notice the influence of our beliefs in all aspects of our lives. Then we can create on earth what we once wanted to ascend *to*.

# Metaphor of Light

THE METAPHOR OF LIGHT, so often used in literature to refer to the divine consciousness, and so often seen in myths, finds an interesting correlation in modern science. Physicist David Bohm speaks of matter as frozen light. Mass is seen as a phenomenon of connecting light rays that go back and forth, "freezing" themselves into a pattern. So physical matter is seen as condensed light moving at average speeds slower than the speed of light. He says, "Light is what enfolds all the universe. In its generalized sense, it is the means by which the entire universe unfolds into itself. It is energy, information, content, form and structure. It is the potential of everything."[4] It would benefit anyone who has the experience of feeling lowered from their divine Source if they would replace the word *lowered* with the word *expanded.* Change the metaphor to reflect the understanding that the supreme Source *expanded* through light into the bioelectromagnetic field around the body and then into the physical body so that the God/Source could have a vehicle to express its light in the physical world.

The metaphors of light, like light itself, abound. It is interesting that the most minute insect is attracted to the light. People in their "after death" experiences speak of going to a light, a light that attracts them. In the mystical traditions light is a common metaphor, and in the Gospel According to Thomas, Nag Hammadi Library,[5] we find many references such as, "I am the light that is above them all, I am the all, the all came forth from me, and the all became me. Cleave the wood, I am there; raise up the

---

[4] *ReVision*, Spring 1983 edition (From an interview with philosopher Renée Weber.) See also footnote 1, chapter 4.
[5] Nag Hammadi Library: Refers to some Gnostic scriptures discovered soon after the end of World War II. The Nag Hammadi "Gnostic Gospels" were discovered in a large storage jar of red claylike material by an Egyptian peasant at the base of the mountain range Jabal al-Tarif near the Nile river in Upper Egypt in 1945. They were in the form of thirteen leather-bound books known as codices and contained fifty-

stone and you will find me." I am convinced that the light we go to in the death experience is the same light we come from and of which we are made.

As will be discussed in Chapter 5, the human body is now seen to be something that processes light biologically in order to live.

Another way to look at this is the human body is the coagulation of the Source consciousness into light and matter, and it is as the temple of the Source within us. We are more than just the consciousness of God/Source" we are also the physical manifestation of it.

As physicist Sir Arthur Eddington said in *The Nature of the Physical World,* " . . .[T]he stuff of the world is mind stuff. . . . Recognizing that the physical world is entirely abstract and without 'actuality' apart from its linkage to consciousness, we restore consciousness to the fundamental position."[6]

In the above sense, then, we are already one with the

---

two separate sections known as tractates and comprised over 1,150 pages. The Library sheds new light on much of the scriptural tradition of Christianity and challenges many beliefs constructed throughout the centuries by the wrangling between leaders in various sects. See also Elaine Pagels' excellent *The Gnostic Gospels* and *Adam, Eve, and the Serpent* (Vintage Press). [6]Cambridge University Press, 1928, pp. 276, 277.

Source we previously thought we needed to ascend to in order to achieve Oneness! Therefore, to repeat in another way, one perspective on the concept of "ascension" is that it essentially refers to an expansion or raising in consciousness.

Simply put, humankind is not less than God; for, as humanity, God/Source is creating and expressing through physical form for the human experience; therefore we must not assume that our power is diminished because we are in human form. This is a crucial point.

In this view it is relatively easy to see that we come to life for fulfillment, to create, to experience, to feel emotions, to understand and to relate to all forms of life and to express this supreme and loving essence that is also ourselves in whatever we do. Therefore, it is not ever purposeful to negate life or our purpose in living in it as less than divine.

Surely, we as humans are indeed the eyes through which God sees Self. Just as surely, the cosmic consciousness that is our Source is manifest as the entire world.

As long as we think
It is only outside of us,
we are only partially using
the full awesomeness of
what we are

Chapter Three

# Could the Source You Pray to Also be You?

*Expressing full potential  / free will  / destiny is choice / what is self? / words, thoughts and manifestation / indiscriminate following of teachers /  the Source outside / giving up to get / time for self / saints and teachers closer to God / expanded perception of God / spirit guides / brilliance of self / God lives! / beyond the karmic wheel / our purpose here.*

I DO NOT THINK THE MEANING AND PURPOSE OF LIFE have ever been kept from us—except by us through our own personally, socially and culturally confined perceptions. Whenever we search *solely outside* ourselves for the way to be in touch with our Source, we unknowingly perpetuate the illusion that we are not *already* in touch. As Meister Eckhart said, "God and I are one in the act of my perceiving him." The very act of searching, instead of experiencing, erroneously perpetuates the notion that we are not already what we are searching for. *Within us are the secrets we are looking for.* . . . Esoteric as this statement may seem, I believe, as we come to the close of this century, it is more and more obvious that the "secrets" of life are not so secret. I feel there is more knowledge in the felt sense of experiencing God than words or years of learning can ever teach. Celebrating and creating in life surely do follow this discovery. As we discover and experiment with ourselves, as scientists measure and hypothesize about the many latent powers that are found within man, we journey further into the experience of the totality of our expression. To begin this we need to establish an ongoing communication with our inner voice and felt essence—which only self can reveal.

Physiologist Dr. Valerie Hunt from the University of California at Los Angeles, in a recorded lecture titled "A Mind Field Model: Biosphere, Cosmosphere Connection" describes what is becoming a more widely accepted view of what it means to be human.[1] At a conference on the ionosphere and cosmosphere, she echoed a statement from Catherine Whiting that "it is easier to study God out there than it is to study God in here." She continued, "It is much easier to study the cosmos out there than it is to study it in here within our

---

[1] "A Mind Field Model" 1987, Bioenergy Fields Foundation, P.O. Box 4234, Malibu, CA 90265

own bodies." She goes on to explain that the biosphere of our own physical bodies contains within it information, or memories of all things that we think make up this biosphere. Some of these beliefs give us difficulty when trying to comprehend our true relationship with the cosmos. She masterfully explains how our biosphere, or unique and personal bioenergetic field, is influenced by and in connection with that of the Earth and all memory. The vibrational frequencies and patterns of our field influence the very way we perceive our world, and, in a kind of feedback loop, our thoughts and perceptions influence us and our biosphere. Dr. Hunt is one of a number of scientists who seem to confirm Russian noblewoman Madame Helena Blavatsky's prediction that twentieth century scientists will propose and explore many of the truths that have heretofore been looked at as esoteric and preserved almost exclusively within the realms of mysticism.

There is a certain profound meaning to be found in Réné Descartes' simple statement, "I think, therefore I am." These words evoke a supreme thought frequency (referring to the fundamental vibrational energy of all things in existence). As discussed in Chapter 2, the duality in life originates when an individual perceives a separation from his or her Source and thinks "I am not" or "I am lower than. . . ." We embrace a sense of unworthiness in life when we feel separated and focus on all we think we are not—all the "not good enoughs"—which perpetuate the self-imposed struggle in life and keep us in a rut in the feedback loop of our own biosphere. It is purposeful to affirm that "I am a physical expression of God, an energy of Its highest frequency of love, intelligence and divinity, and am therein worthy to experience the support of the whole of the cosmos and universal mind.... I acknowledge that it is a natural state for me that I am in open receivership and supported in life for the fulfillment of self, and that my personality-self and God-self, are all in harmony in the fulfillment of the creativity of self."

# Expressing Full Potential

IN MANY BRAINSTORMING SESSIONS and my interviews with world renowned scientists, philosophers and theologians, I have noted a continually reemerging question that ultimately remains unanswered: "If indeed we are in the oneness of God, as many believe we are, why haven't we been living as such, and why isn't it more obvious...?" Interestingly, perhaps we *are* living as such, and maybe it *is* obvious, but the commoness of it obscures its profundity.

I propose that the belief systems we have acquired throughout milleniums of our history, as suggested in Chapter One and later in this Chapter, rather than clarifying, have perpetuated the lingering sense that we are but "mere mortals" influenced by everything outside of us—stars, nature, earth, religous authorities, etc. We have relied upon these outside forces rather than our own powerful and innate free will and wisdom, which is our heritage from a powerful and undefined life Source. It is quite reasonable to discuss how we, expressing the power of this Source, influence everything in our lives, from our relationships, careers, abundance or lack of it and even our health.

# Free Will

HOW COULD THAT BE? We have free will to choose our life course because we were honored to be equal, one and the same as the Source which shares it with us. As such, free will is our inherited right, and our thought is therefore supreme. We create, through our own beliefs, thoughts and attitudes, our experiences in life. This fact is so fundamental that it is obscured by its very simplicity. With free will we create, through the power of thought. Controversial though it may seem, I believe circumstances in our life reflect back to us what we think of ourselves. This fascinating idea—that of free will and co-equality— has been explored for centuries, and it, as well as the beliefs which prohibit one from recognizing the obvious influence one has on one's life, will be examined further in chapters 6 on "Oneness" and 7 on "The Universal Mind: Exploring Conscious Interconnectedness."

The more we love the God Source and the more we love and honor It within us, the more both become nurtured. The more both are nurtured, the more awesome and unlimited is our desire and ability to create. What we do with this awareness, in our given professions or personal lives, may then be done with greater excellence. Our power to do this is in our own hands, in our own free will and thought.

This realization is very much needed—and is being currently addressed everywhere in the world. In recent years almost every major newspaper in the country has doubled the size of its "Life" or "Living" section. The publishing industry reflects this wide-spread interest in books and magazines about self-help, health, psychology, metaphysics and the "new age."

Discussion of the potential within us all raises many questions about destiny, purpose and personal enlightenment. What I mean by enlightenment is conscious acknowledgement, or greater awareness of Self, beginning with one's own individual impact on all of life. Suffice it to say here, we don't have to give up, overcome or negate our humanness. We only have to realize and allow ourselves to be fulfilled wherever we are, in whatever situation. One can have children, lovers, wealth and be whatever one wants in the marketplace or community, whatever serves one and brings joy and fulfillment. There is no need for "sacrificing" anything to obtain favor from anyone. Life is already sacred, and so are we.

# Destiny is Choice

CAREFUL SCRUTINY SHOWS THAT all teachings about enlightenment, sooner or later, must always come back to one's self.

These teachings are not about the ancient mystery schools, nor are they only about Jesus or other prophets, saints and sages themselves. *Such teachings are never about the messenger;* they are about the Divine Self of you and me. I believe, of all that has ever been taught of self-mastery or God, that, in part, a key to understanding it in its most simple yet self-empowering truth, is to know one shares with the "Beloved Father" the power of thought. This is how one co-creates all of one's tomorrows. What we call luck and good fortune is therefore self-created, and *our destiny is our choice.*

It is ironic, in view of all the spiritual searching seemingly done by many over the ages, that all one needs do in order to know the Source one seeks is, as was inscribed over the door of Delphi long before Jesus: "Know yourself!"

This fact of the power of our thoughts is further borne out by many of our scientists who have found that each thought we have affects us in some way, not only in the individual vibrational biosphere, but also in the physical body. These scientists have now discovered that we cannot have a thought without it having some effect on our bodies, at the very least at a molecular level. For example, compare the work of, among others, Candace Pert, Chief of the section on brain biochemistry in the Clinical Neuroscience Branch at the National Institute of Mental Health. Among other discoveries it has been found that hormones in the body and cells in the immune system and brain are linked in such a way that researchers can "no longer make a strong distinction between the brain and the body." Noting the bias in the Western idea that consciousness is totally in "the head," Pert states, "I believe the research findings I have described indicate that we need to start thinking about how consciousness can project into the body."[2]

# What is Self?

WHAT IS SELF? and how do we know it? Those are perennial questions. The ultimate question is, "How does one know and master oneself?" One way is to observe one's own effect on one's life. For instance, if there is a doubt that you know how to manifest, or how to use the will to create into being, observe your life experience, observe your thoughts and the words you

---

[2] See interview in *Woman of Power*, No. 11, 1988 "Science and Technology."

speak. You may recognize them as they are mirrored back to you through the varied experiences of your life. This is something that requires contemplation and self focus. Take some time here and think of an example in your life. For instance, how is it that you acquired your particular job, your relationship, your state of health and so on? Did these events occur against your will? Or, was an unspoken wish from your own deep desire what manifested for you? Try tracing any of your life events back to your self.

Many feel that there are unseen forces in the universe that are more powerful than we are. I believe, conversely, that we are so powerful, through the free will of self, that even those of the so-called "unseen omnipotence" cannot create anything in our own personal lives against our will. I feel that ancient prophets, masters and inspired ones come most graciously and lovingly to teach us about ourselves through our desire to know, and they can therefore endeavor to assist us to embrace the unlimitedness of what we are, but they cannot do anything either against our will or without our willing.

# Words, Thoughts and Manifestation

TO REITERATE, EVEN IF WE THINK we of ourselves do not manifest, or create, it is validating and important to know that we have co-created and do co-create our future. Our destiny unfolds for us, and what we call good fortune, wellness or lack of it, abundance or suffering, are created from our thoughts—which go wherever we project them. I realize that for some this may be a controversial thought, but I strongly believe that we often run amuck *because we are not well aware of what we think* and therefore have little awareness of how powerful our thoughts are in creating. This is a very simple part of life—and a very important one.

# Indiscriminate Following of Teachers

I KNOW that to acknowledge one's self and all one's power seems far more difficult than being taught by someone who seems knowledgeable about us and our potentials. While this can be beneficial, an important consideration is to look at how the action of going from one teacher to another for self-assurance—without discrimination—can actually perpetuate the attitude that one does not already know or have available within oneself the knowledge one seeks.

Indiscriminate following of spiritual teachers can give one the illusion of spiritual progress, which in fact may be a diversion from the very core self of you you seek to explore and know. This is especially true when the focus is inappropriately placed on the teacher.

Self-examination and personal participation in one's

own development are of great importance. My experiences have proven that well-centered spiritual teachers would never encourage any adulation of their own self, but would rather focus on the empowerment of the Source-self that is within all.

I believe we all know for ourselves about ourselves, and if we understand this and practice how we can better monitor and master ourselves, we will see that all of our potential is *already within* waiting for us to discover it. We will further explore the profound implications of this, as it applies both personally and as a society.

At this juncture, it might be rather fun, and perhaps instructive, to take a global overview of some of the various cultural myths and metaphors that have made their way into the thinking and belief systems of modern society.

## The Source Outside

AS I MENTIONED in chapter 1, the perception that God is very much outside of the world prevailed for early humankind. [SEE FIG. 1] Many prayed, danced or chanted so that this Source would show grand favor upon them in their life, to give abundance, to help in the growth of crops, to please stop the rain, to allow the love of another to come to them. Many people prayed to this Source

In the beginning of humankind's evolution, through the time of the  Newtonian views of the world, there was a God perceived to be separate from physical life:   duality.

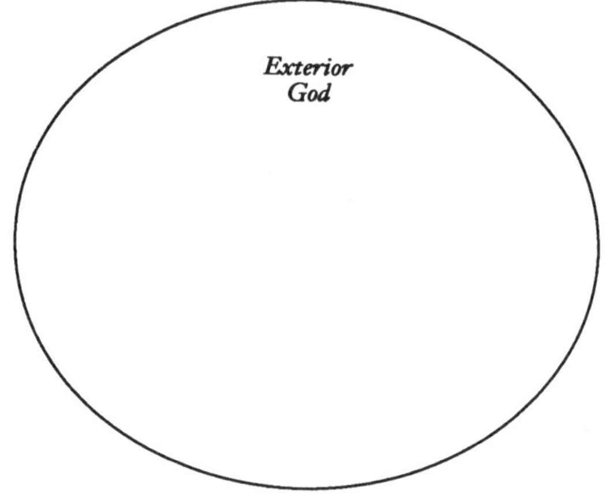


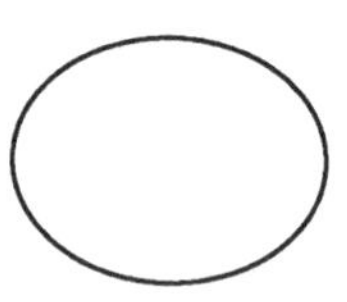

*Humankind as lowered from  God*

**Fig. 1**

outside them, and to the degree that they felt they were worthy of their request, the prayer was answered. Of course, if the prayer was not answered, then the feeling occurred that they were not worthy, or had done something "wrong," or perhaps rationalized their undesireable circumstances as something they thought they needed to learn from or overcome. All through this they did not realize that it was their own divine influence, as expressed through their own free will, that gave or took away.

Now of course it is being proposed—and for some, argued—that our thoughts of worthiness or unworthiness are determined by us, and such is the nature of "God" that our will and thoughts are honored, respected or allowed. There is no judgment and no reward from an outside Source alone. All is an adventure or experience in the great interplay of life.

# Giving Up to Get

THOSE who worshipped a separate God would sacrifice to show the absoluteness of their love for this Source, for they felt It was an awesome God with awesome power, because in their view It created all things that could be seen. Many in this belief system created rules that they could have a little of something, but not too much. Sacrifices were offered to express the degree of their earnestness in having their God give blessing and favor.

Sacrifice has been erroneously understood for so long as a way to honor God, not only in pagan times, but even in later times, and even today. Today some are still willing to give up, to struggle, to do anything in order to earn this God's favor. This is often a very subtle personal and at times subconscious belief for many people, and some will do almost anything for this favor, save to love this Source as within self and each other, and to *embrace with joy the gift of Life.*

# Time for Self

IT IS IMPORTANT to allow quiet spaces in your life where you can experience being filled with the calm and unspoken sense of being alive. *The action of creating this space in life is of great importance.* As a grand teacher once said to me, "Schedule yourself into your life." My first response was, "I am too busy. I don't have enough time for everything that I need to accomplish now." My thoughts were, "I must . . . , I should. . . , I'm expected to. . . . I ought to do this, etc. . . ."

He repeated, "Schedule yourself in; take time—alone time—for self."

When I did, I realized I had created an open space that filled me with the sense of being alive—that subtle, joyous feeling that I remember as a child when I had the playtime and the space to feel it constantly. This energized my whole being and all my activities when I resumed them. I had forgotten about this as an adult.

When I again remembered this, I felt rejuvenated, and all the things I had to achieve and accomplish were more swiftly and creatively done in less time than I had become used to spending. In fact, during one of these sojourns, I wrote two songs, both of which were later recorded.[3]

I now have no guilt or feeling of "should have" during these inner moments. I now accomplish more in less time.

It truly is that effortless to embrace with joy the gift of life!  Certainly it is to this purpose that we are here.

Since understanding where we have been often frees

---

[3] "It is in the word unspoken/The dreamer feels her way/For life is full of answers /In the quiet of the day/And so it goes on flowing/Your life is but your dream/So dream, my sweet lady/It's your kingdom, you're the Queen/So dream sweet dreams/Don't let the world get in your way/Don't get lost in your tomorrows/Live only for today/So find your place with nature/For it's there you'll learn to be/For life is full of living/It's there for you and me/Knowing your deep feelings/With thoughts received and sent/And your life goes on unfolding/And all you've known is just a hint." *The Dreamer*, Platinum International Music, Preston/Ratner Publishers.

As Humankind evolved in understanding:
Exterior
God
Saints, teachers
and guides
Humankind
still separate and
lowered from
God

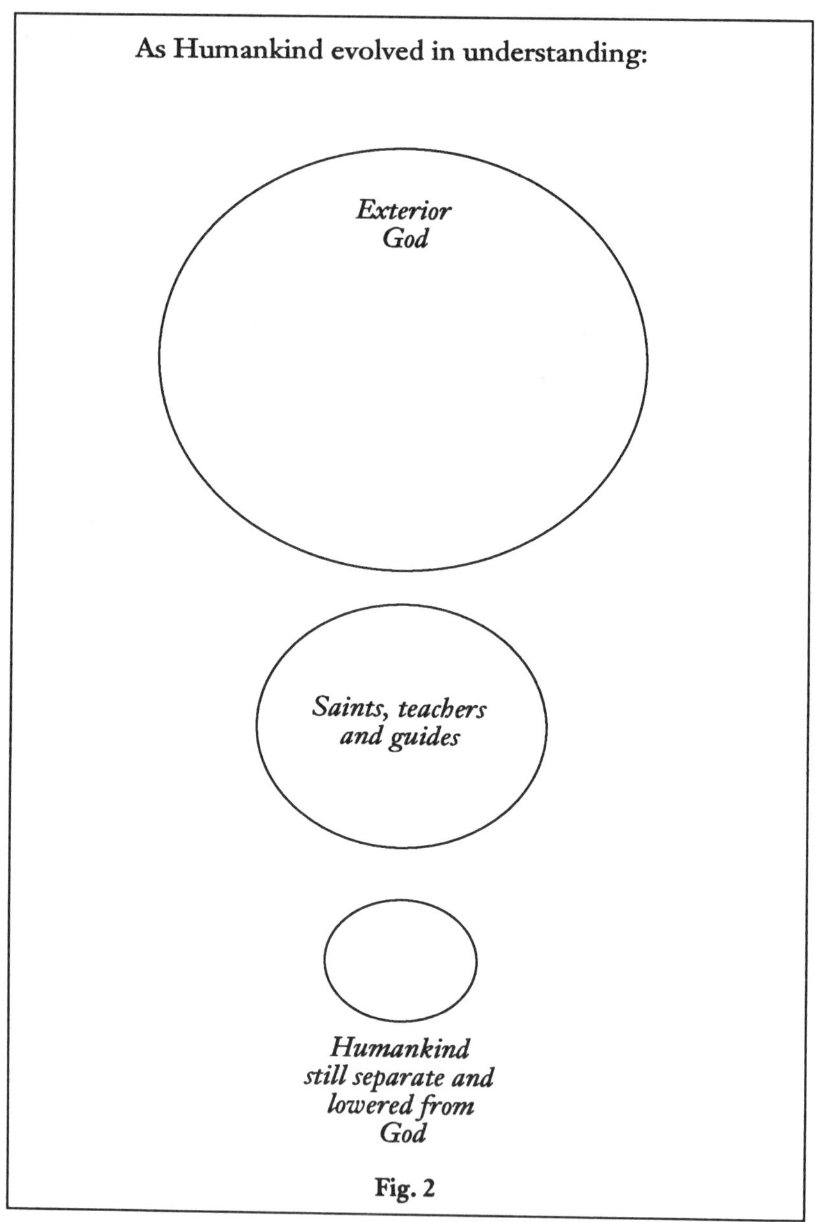

Fig. 2

the spirit, I would like to continue to explore the overview history of our efforts to relate to our Source.

## Saints, Teachers Closer to God

OVER the centuries interpretations have evolved. By encapsulating time, we can see that gradually, through this expanding consciousness, people began to allow themselves to associate humanness more with God. [SEE FIG. 2] For some, perceptions were expanded to include saints—those who were also of the flesh but who had become more God-like in the peoples' understanding. In this belief humankind became more like the image of God. Some believed that if they placed the medallion or *cartouche* or symbol of the saint upon their body, they were protected by its spirit, or its blessing. Even though the people allowed that saints could become Godlike, they developed beliefs that saints therefore became less human, and rules were formed that certain human activities and privileges had to be denounced, overcome or forfeited in order for anyone to achieve this status.

As some people expanded their perspective, they began to allow themselves to be guided by those referred to as spiritual teachers. Many of a more mystical inclination embraced spirit guides[4] who they believed had evolved

---

[4] Those who after death of the physical body are perceived to have entered a "higher" realm, "closer" to God, thus allowing them to be of greater assistance to man.

and who had once lived and gained *favor* from God. Many people sought the help of these spirit guides for they still perceived themselves as lesser or separate—a truth empowered by their belief in it. [SEE FIG. 3] In places this belief included the concept that evolution to God occurs during the process of reincarnations.

How does one get beyond this "wheel," or "spiral effect," concepts that describe using the process of incarnation as a cycle to evolve spiritually to go eventually to God? How does one go beyond this cycle of repeated incarnations endeavoring to "become," instead of simply embracing one's divine heritage?

Let's first examine the notion that there are unseen spirits whose help people need in order to embrace that they are also the "God" they seek. I acknowledge there can certainly be these teachers and guides that are in a realm "separate" from us, that love us and desire to assist us. However, I also believe there is more of that truth to understand. . . . This will be addressed in this chapter in the section "Beyond the Karmic Wheel."

# Expanded Perception of God

CONTINUING with this historical view of beliefs, evolution advanced and many expanded their beliefs to include a "higher self." They perceived this higher self to have a

As Humankind spiritually developed, perception
allowed this:

God as
Thought/Consciousness,
but still an exterior Source

Allowing self to be
more God-like, closer
because of
saints, higher self,
guides and teachers.

Humankind as
still separate from
God however

Fig. 3

greater overview. They believed it was closer to God than familiar self. As they accessed this higher self through meditation, contemplation or prayer, they gained insight, clarity and input to assist them. However, if there are those who do not acknowledge the higher self, teachers or saints, then they still may be praying to a separate entity, this force called God that serves humankind. This raises an interesting question. How is it that all these prayers are answered?

The prayers are "answered" because consciousness as God, higher self and humankind are not all separate, or divided. In an expanded understanding of all these truths …we are ultimately one. As physicist Sir Arthur Eddington so well said, "When the electron vibrates, the universe shakes." So, it is with the whole of consciousness, which is totally interconnected.

In a simple view, within us is simultaneously the Light and the consciousness of God expressed as humankind. [SEE FIG. 4] Metaphorically speaking, the God/Source took the adventure into light, our light body, and continued the adventure into matter, our physical body.

To reiterate, the very Source, the very Light that many want to go to is now clearly seen to be where we are already. *As long as we think It is only outside of us, we are only partially using the full awesomeness of what we are.*

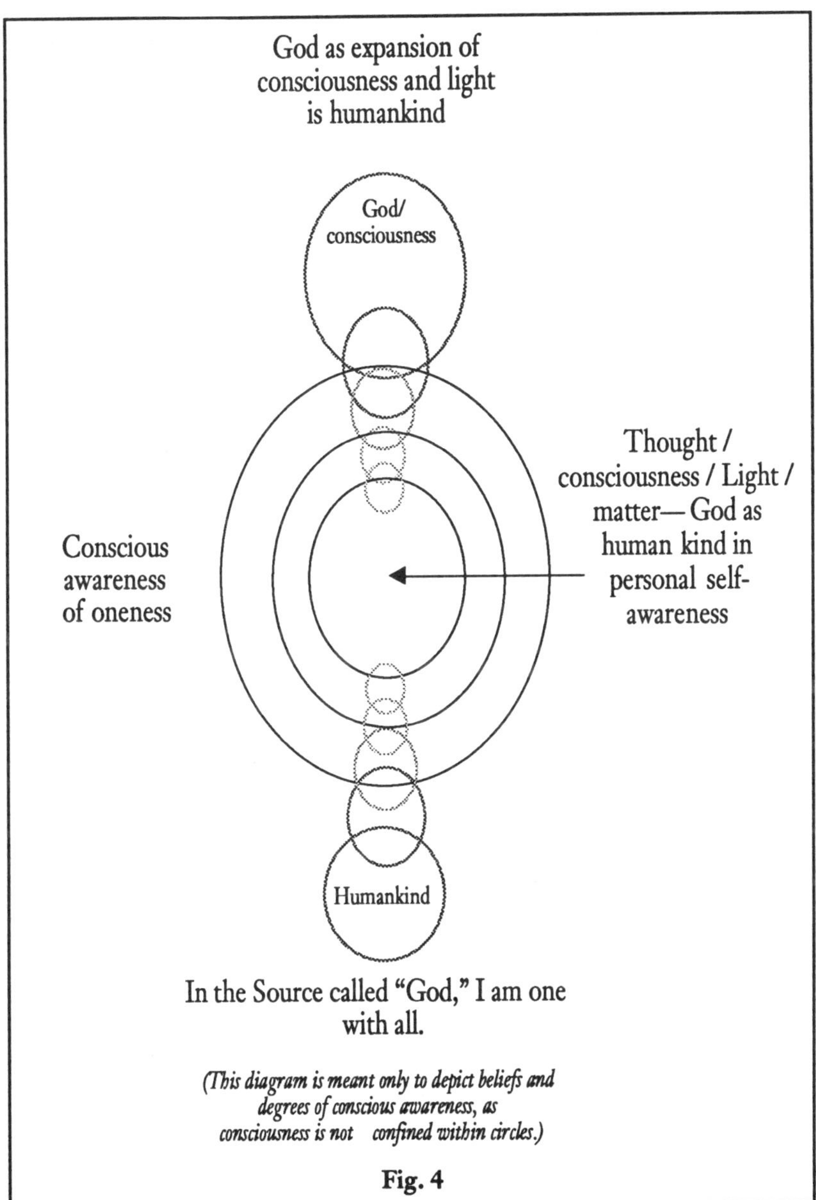

God as expansion of
consciousness and light
is humankind
God/
consciousness
Thought /
consciousness / Light /
matter— God as
human kind in
personal self-
awareness
Conscious
awareness
of oneness
Humankind
In the Source called "God," I am one
with all.
(This diagram is meant only to depict beliefs and
degrees of conscious awareness, as
consciousness is not   confined within circles.)

**Fig. 4**

# Spirit Guides

I FEEL there is some value and insight in a side note here to further explore the subject of religious saints and spiritual guides.

There are those who never embraced the mystical concept of guide or teacher. They remained satisfied with their belief in saints and separate God. Of these, some continued to go to religious leaders in hopes they would speak in good favor to this God for them. Still others began to embrace that they had a spiritual guide or a teacher. They believed the more that they embraced this and allowed their consciousness to expand and acknowledge these guides and teachers, the more help they would receive.

An important question arises here. One person gets spiritual advice from exterior sources and another from internal. How and why would both of these, as well as all the vastly different beliefs in the world be served? It is because the creating consciousness and beliefs of those individuals willed and thus engaged the desired validation of their beliefs. . . . Through the Source known as God, any desire to receive is as equally honored and supported within any belief system as is the desire not to receive.

Compare this statement from Willis Harman in "Create Your Future," from the Institute of Noetic

Sciences: "Within a couple of decades it will be widely accepted that inner conscious awareness is a cause of reality in the universe and our daily lives." Once again it is relevant to note that everything as we experience it in the world *is a reflection of the thought/consciousness of its origin.* In the act of embracing the totality of what we are, we can break from the common thought that only what we see exists, and we can begin to explore more of life.

# Brilliance of Self

THERE is an important point that remains to be explored about the concept of higher self. Before anyone acknowledged a higher self, how did this self communicate to them? Though many people believed in metaphysical guides, they had not yet allowed their perception of higher self to exist. Could it be that their inner guide or teacher was their higher self, who wholly knew that their acknowledgement of it as part of them was not acceptable to them as yet? Therefore it would project upon them perhaps as an old Indian, a wise old woman or an Oriental sage, so that they would embrace this information. Perhaps at that time they preferred this view because they had the attitude that if this communication came from outside of them, it was far more credible than if it was from self.

Many readers may have had an experience like this, and may have wondered why they were not scared, but instead felt rather safe, even comfortable and loved. As stated above, this communication may have been from a particular identity, or aspect of self that would project back onto them so as to ensure their receptivity, and this personification was as well a reminder of some wisdom from a memory of a life that they had lived.

My experience and investigation indicate that we are very multidimensional in our consciousness, a fact medical doctors, psychologists and other scientists are well aware of. We are so very brilliant, that we can create whatever we need to mirror back to and thereby teach ourselves. It is not a separate higher self, but the emergence of a greater awareness of our God self, which projects back on us an identity or a message we will embrace to support and assist us in our life. Many embrace that assistance because it is comfortable or familiar and feels true. As we grow in awareness and understand the awesomeness of who we are, we begin to understand that we are all these things and much, much more.

# God Lives!

WHERE else, and through whom else would the Source we are feel the embrace of a young child's arms around the neck of its parent, the wind as it blows through one's hair, the fragrance of a flowering rose, the tenderness of the experience of childbirth and the understanding that is exchanged between glances of two strangers as they pass on a busy street.

Where else can the experience be found, save in us, of the music of the world, the choir of a thousand voices in song as they join in a holiday, the joy in the reunion of a family that gathers for a birth, a holiday or a marriage, the crispness of the fall air, the warmth of sun across the bare shoulders of a man as he works on the land, as well as the sense of creative accomplishment as the artist or musician finishes a piece of work!

# Beyond the Karmic Wheel

ALTHOUGH people of certain cultures thought that if they could reincarnate and come back and overcome what they did before in previous lives—which is what is sometimes called karma—they would gradually make progress and they could journey further out on the spiral wheel until they were higher/closer to God. They believed that to the degree they advanced, they could incarnate each time at a higher level. They did not yet realize that all this occured within their mind-set. *In actuality, at anytime they could have evoked a conscious realization that they were already one with what they wanted to evolve to.*

Another point to be explored in conjunction with this belief is that there are entities who believe that while they are in spirit form waiting to incarnate they can choose to work off karma by functioning as a spirit guide, or a teacher in order to come back in life at a higher level. Through the *desire* of many people for guidance, disembodied entities could access, through thought frequency, *receptive* people, such as in mediumship and psychic channeling, which is widely known today. Therein they could become guides and teachers from time to time in order to earn good karma. Although from their point of view they could guide, it is important to realize they were not yet themselves necessarily *fully* realized. They are most loving, caring, even helpful, but limited, and they often *unknowingly* perpetuate the illusion of separateness and the need for an arduous journey of becoming. On the other hand, if an entity can teach from the highest perspective and overview of all Reality, then obviously it has come to the fully realized condition. Thus it would behoove anyone following any such entities to discern what they are teaching. . . .

Spirit entities are not to be seen necessarily as more greatly evolved beings, nor are they to be presumed to have always more wisdom. In some cases they may have broad views, but it is for each individual to determine the value of those views. For if the entities are upon a limited wheel of understanding, they can only guide you within that wheel or belief system.

Nevertheless, this seems an appropriate place to elaborate on terms often used in spiritual circles, *angels* and *light-workers*. Having received many blessings from them, I am one of the first to acknowledge the many benefits that often come to us from them. On numerous occasions I have been both blessed and honored by their assistance. This is why I advocate discernment in these matters. The assistance offered to us may be of differing value and come from spiritual guides of differing levels of enlightenment and consciousness. It is always useful to use reason and intellect for evaluation.

## Kingdom of Heaven

If, as scriptures and sacred doctrines have stated, the kingdom of heaven is indeed within, then it is not "out," "up," or somewhere else. It must be perceived first in the field of consciousness, which enhances an individual's attitude. Thus the "kingdom of heaven" can be viewed, created and experienced as a part of life.

It is hard to estimate, as the story of notes in a jar in chapter 1 indicates, how many people feel life is a struggle. I firmly believe that we truly need to first love ourselves and love life and honor the simple truth that we chose to be here in life. This will eliminate the dual thought that says, "I don't honor that I am here. This must be a mistake. I'd rather be somewhere else." I've heard many people express the view that they think it's better out there in the unseen or on another planet, or in the afterlife. If they think it's better out there what are they saying about here and their choice to be here? It bears repeating that it is *attitude* that makes life here common and obscures the miracle that it is..., for surely the cosmic consciousness that is our Source is manifest as the entire world.

# Our Purpose Here

WITHOUT exception, I believe our purpose in life is to aspire to live joyously and harmoniously. We are here to celebrate life not to endure and overcome it. I feel we are creative beings expressing in physical form the Divine Essence. I do not see God as being a confined Source; I see It, rather, as an ever-expanding and creative energy that is an ongoing process...*and therefore so are we!* Could the original dream, the original will and desire, the ultimate gift to our Source be that we would express our selves unlimitedly in life?

This is quite different than thinking the goal is to overcome life as a challenge, instead of a loving, creative experience of creation in coexistence. I feel that if we leave life without fulfilling our realization of it, we will be *self-driven* to return again so as to experience fulfilment. There is really no outer journey to God ... there is only the inner journey of expanded awareness. Rather than search for the meaning *of* life, look for meaning *in* life.

I believe we are both challenged and encouraged to

learn through increased conscious awareness to create our preferred reality . . . and therefore preferred future. Whether our life is experienced as heaven or hell is a reflection of our level of consciousness and perception of self, through which we then create our own reality and our shared world. As a master once said, *The degree to which we love, honor and master the totality of who we are, is the degree that we will create heaven on earth.*

Our free will is awesome, and our
thoughts are like jewels

*As Brahman [ God ] constitutes a person's Self it is not something to be attained by that person. . . ; for as it is omnipresent it is part of its nature that it is ever present to everyone.* —*Shankara*, Vedanta Sutras of Badarayana

## Chapter Four

# The Awesomeness of You

*Journey of creation / light body / validation, intuition and personal genius / infinite mind / thoughts and words as prayers / change and repositioning / change, the unknown and steadfastness / repositioning to receive / judgment, observation and discernment / mirroring to one another/ religion called "becoming"*

THERE IS A MYTH that we were the spirits or souls who journeyed from consciousness into matter for the unlimited expression in life as human beings. In this journey of creation, we formed humanity. . . . Therefore, we must be vastly loved and cherished by the very Source from which we and all creation stem. This says a great deal about us that bears continued examination.

We are creative beings, and through the body we express as such in this miracle of life and breath. *We are the very miracle that we've been looking for,* and the degree to which we see ourselves separate from God is the degree that we then suffer the dualities that are created, all from our feeling of separateness. Remember that this duality is a human-created illusion. Since we created this illusion, it is within our power to reverse it through the acknowledgement that it is only humankind who sees itself separate from its Source.

# Light Body

ARTISTS since antiquity have painted religious or enlightened masters with a halo or aura, endeavoring to depict the glow of their "light body," which must have been more easily *felt* than seen.

Matter, as physicist David Bohm has said, is light at a slower speed. Within every cell of the body dwells the light and life energy of our God/Source, which also is the light that encompasses our bodies and is referred to as our light body. I believe this light aura emanates from everyone and even more strongly from anyone who facilitates, through thought and feeling, the realization of the light/Source that we all are. One result of this realization is that the light of the body is more fully activated, that is to say, it takes on a higher vibrational frequency and may then be perceived or felt by others.

Theoretical physicists Bob Tolpen and Fred Alan Wolfe have said that:

> The speculation that matter may be nothing but trapped light energy arises from the famous Einstein formula $E=Mc^2$, which equates energy, $E$, and matter, $M$, by multiplying the latter by the speed of light, $c$, twice. Physicists have observed this formula in action in the process known as electron-positron annihilation and in the inverse process known as electron-positron creation. What happens is that an electron … collides with its antimatter self, the positron, and both vanish, leaving two particles of light called photons.[1]

Marilyn Ferguson, in commenting on the theories of Arthur Young on evolution, and Frank Barr, M.D., on the role of the melanin molecule in the human body says:

> [L]ight energy structures matter; that is, matter is organized through the interaction of molecules composed of slowed-down light. These molecular combinations 'eat' light in order to maintain, expand and evolve matter. The more highly evolved a species, the more complex its biological capacity to use light. Human beings, according to the model, move toward the freedom of the photon itself, through their increasingly subtle structure.[2]

---

[1]*Space-Time and Beyond* (Bantam Books 1975, rev. ed. 1982).
[2] Arthur Young's theory of evolution and M.D. Frank Barr's theory about the role of the body's melanin molecule in organizing living systems. (*Brain/Mind Bulletin*, V. 8, Nos. 12/13)

---

In this regard I would like to draw your attention to a statement in the *Gospel According to Thomas* of the Nag-Hammadi Library when, speaking to his disciples, Jesus said,

> If they say to you: "From where are your origins?" say to them, "We have come from the Light, where the Light has begun through itself." (50) [3]

How interesting that many were told over two thousand years ago what modern science now confirms. . . further demystifying our place of origin—*we are all of the Light.*

# Validation, Intuition and Personal Genius

AS A WISE PROPHET ONCE SAID, "I laugh when I see that the fish in the water are thirsty. . . ." This quote reminds me of how we, throughout the history of our race, have witnessed great thinkers and visionaries—and today leading scientists—who, through their teachings *validate the divinity which before we only suspected in our quiet moments.*

In consciousness there is therefore light, and in it

---

[3] The number in parentheses refers to the number of the saying in the Gospel.

there is a life force energy that exists in all things. Through the vibrational frequency of the atoms and molecules in our bodies we are electromagnetic beings.[4] We send out frequencies from the body with our thoughts.

Among the infinite possibilites from these thoughts there is the fact that we can thereby attract or draw to us information that begins to validate anything we want, including that *we are in fact more than physical matter.* We attract information from the Source by our will to know more, which emanates out through thought frequency and draws in greater knowledge and life events, continually creating life adventures for us to explore. This could be why, when we *wish* to draw to ourselves information in books or other sources, that world literature is seemingly written or discovered simultaneously as the desire arises in people. In turn, we participate, through our intent and desire, in drawing this knowledge in, and others who are in tune create with or express it.

Perhaps you've noticed certain trends in films, music or literature and thought to yourself, "I just thought about that!" or "I just had a dream about that very thing!" This is not unlike thinking of someone who then all of a sudden telephones you or whom you may unexpectedly meet on the street. This is all taking place within a mind

---

[4] See, among other books *The Body Electric: Electromagnetism and the Foundation of Life*, by Robert O. Becker, M.D. and Gary Selden. (Quill, William Morrow, 1985)

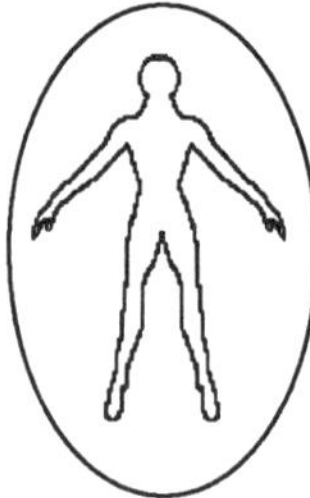

In previous beliefs the body was solid, surrounded by a limited field, or aura.

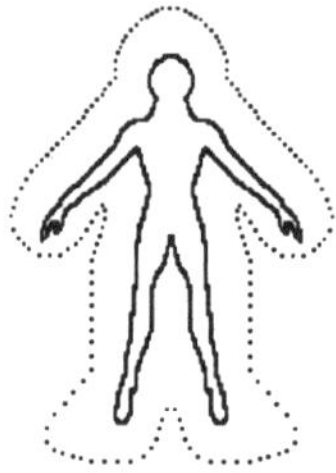

In expanded views the body is surrounded by a permeable and dynamic field that resonates with others' bio-fields and all fields in existence.

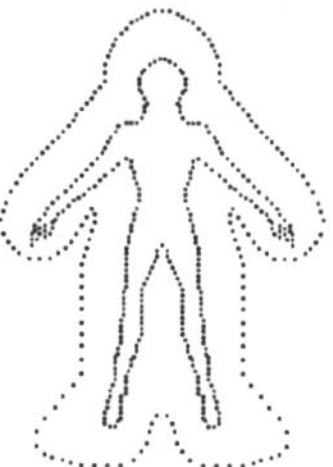

With the views of modern physics, the physical brain/body is also seen as non-solid, dynamic and, through its electro-magnetic properties, interactive with all bio-fields.

We are not confined or restricted only within our "own" energy field, but rather ongoingly contributing to and accessing from the collective consciousness.

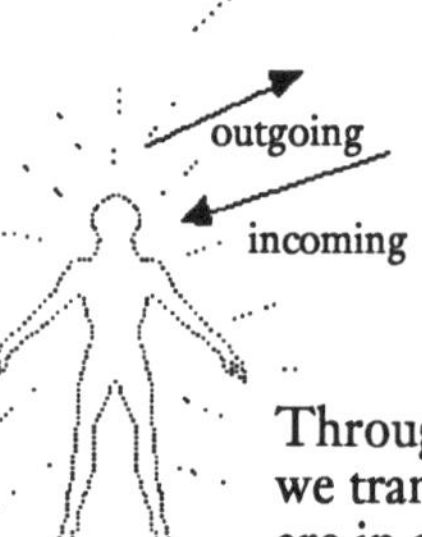


Through the thought waves we transmit and receive we are in a form of continuous communication with the "God Source," All That Is.

**Fig. 5**

field, or unified force. As physicist and psychologist Buryl Payne states, *"Force* is a term applied when matter is set in motion. By this principle, thought must be given a place beside gravity, electricity, magnetism, and spin as a fundamental force."[5] This point of view also supports the preceding (and ensuing) discussion on the value of mastering one's words and thoughts.

# Infinite Mind

THE fact that thought is a force with electromagnetic properties gives new meaning and credibility to the role of intuition—to the value to be found in exploring and developing our intuitive sense. More of the information we want and need may be accessed from the universal and infinitely expanding consciousness within the mind of God. This Mind is sure to hold great and miraculous wonders and enrichments that are yet to be fully enjoyed and known to us. [SEE FIG. 5] Developed intuition gives way to original thought and allows the development of personal genius which in turn allows one to go beyond the limits inherent in social consciousness and to access the expanded level of consciousness often referred to as "the Christ" or "Buddhahood," or cosmic and higher consciousness.

---

[5]*The Body Magnetic* (Academy for Peace Research, 1988, p. 76)

---

# Thoughts and Words as Prayers

WHAT do affirming, meditating, kneeling in prayer and cursing in anger all have in common? . . . They all manifest!

Our free will is awesome, and our thoughts are like jewels. No one else's thoughts are more powerful than our own. Scriptural evidence shows that Buddha, Jesus and other illuminated ones transcended any doubt in their consciousness as to their own origin and worthiness, when they embraced the full power of their existence in and of "God." The full force of this power is engaged within them, just as it is waiting to be engaged in us. They knew that every day is a Sabbath and every word is a prayer—every one of them.

We also can and must learn more about our thoughts and how to master them, so that as our life unfolds and reflects back to us, we can recognize the very thoughts that created the life scenario that is ours. Perhaps this mastery could be the very action we all need in order to create and experience the heaven on earth we all seek. The more one embraces this understanding, the more one will increasingly speak as a master who knows that words manifest.

*Each day we live and every word we speak contributes in various ways to our own experienced reality.*

# Change and Repositioning

IT IS COUNTERPRODUCTIVE to project a positive thought one day for what you want and the next day damn the very events that happen to bring that desire to you. Such contradictory thoughts block your ability to receive your request. It is more productive to project forward what you want and allow the repositioning of yourself for receivership of your desire. Practice affirming that what you want can, and will manifest . . . regardless of how it may appear in the moment. Observe the events that begin to take place in your life as a result of your desire for change. Often the events are subtle, but unawareness of, or a rejection of them is to negate the change you desired.

Difficult though it may seem, there is reason to develop faith and have confidence, for when we call out, as many do, to the greaterness of ourselves, to the universe—Divine Source—that we want or desire something, assistance, change in our lives and so on, we activate a greater, more knowing part of ourselves.

This more knowing aspect of our personal psyche is aware of even more than what we might ask for in our limited consciousness. We need to *trust*, therefore, if we call forth for a desire within us to be fulfilled, that it will come to pass. Remember, nothing outside of us grants or denies, for the God/Source supports our attitudes—we determine for ourselves.

# Change,
# the Unknown and Steadfastness

AS THE CHANGE or repositioning which you are actually calling forth occurs in your life, it may not look or appear to be what you wanted. This is the point when most become discouraged or frightened and rationalize that they do not want what they asked for, because as it begins to come, it changes their familiar reality. They do not know what that will be like. They do know what the present is like, even if it is suffering; at least it is familiar, and they have learned to survive in this understanding. As change starts to occur, it signifies the unknown, and many start to become concerned. This is the time when they are not in mastery of their thought or emotion; they start to reposition, but they now perceive themselves to be in a limbo state between what they did have and what they want, and they begin to panic and lose their focused thought; this is when they compromise their desires and potentials.

If you fit in this description, try instead to remain steadfast to the ideal, so that it can come all the way to fruition; then you can reposition yourself to receive your goal, all the way into and through change. Expect change to come if you ask for something you don't already have, for it will take that change to bring forth into your life an ideal you are not already experiencing. Instead of "change," it may help to call it "repositioning" in order to be in receivership of what you called forth and proclaimed that you desired as an ideal.

# Repositioning to Receive

THOSE WHO ASK for something to change in their lives, but who fear the change are like a small child upon an embankment who casts forth a string and a hook into the river to catch a fish. There is the child's will, which is like the water that moves his line further down. The child realizes that he placed his line one place in the river, but the flow of the river has repositioned the line and hook further downstream. That isn't where he put it in, and in resisting the natural flow, and thinking that the fish is only where he put his hook in, he pulls the line out before he catches the fish! Resisting the change, or repositioning, he pulls out his hook, he withdraws his desire instead of trusting that it could bring him what he wants.

So, as a repositioning occurs, do not go into past or limited thought or fear of the change, but stay aligned. Say to yourself, "I am being repositioned from the calling forth of my ideal, and I will allow myself to be in receivership," and maintain that affirmative thought until you have received what you desired. You have to keep faith that when you speak a proclamation to the universe, or the greater part of yourself, it is definitely on its way to you. Regardless of how it looks to you based on your past understanding of the world, go with your positive feelings and desires and pull into your world of everyday life what it is you truly want.

# Judgment,
# Observation and Discernment

HAVE YOU EVER WONDERED about all the rules in life and worried about breaking some of them? The older I got and the more rules I learned, the more I realized that the rules simply created additional ways for me to judge myself or others who didn't appear to be living these same rules. Then I would judge myself for judging them . . . sound like a familiar cycle?

This begs the question "What is judgment?" Ultimately, for my own peace of mind, I had to learn that in judging others I was making them either right or wrong. Finally, I found I could observe someone who may be doing something I did not want to do, but that didn't necessarily make them wrong. It was simply my own observation and preference. One way wisdom is acquired is through observing and cumulatively gaining the wisdom of the observation. To formulate an opinion on what you observe results in gained insight and the development of more wisdom, which gives you an overview whereby you can look at any given circumstance and reason why one person did this and another one did that. You know through the experience that these actions create certain results. Personal observation of what is around you in nature, plants and animals, as well as others, is a grand and simple way to learn.

When we take our creative and powerful thoughts and make something an absolute, whether right or wrong, we thus *limit ourselves* to that particular opinion or judgment—we thus limit our ability to reason its relativity and changeability. It is important to consider that we are always subject to our own limited beliefs, *thus when we judge we create more ways for ourselves to be judged within those beliefs.* When we cease the need to make others right or wrong, greater or lesser, and simply see life as the unlimited and varied adventure it is, we gain more understanding and an increased ability to joyfully interact with others. This is why we've always been encouraged not to judge.

## Mirroring to One Another

THERE is also a reflecting or mirroring aspect to judgment. In psychological theory, and in some spiritual teachings, there is a concept regarding the mirroring of certain personality and behavioral traits. This mirroring effect assists people to be aware of their own actions as seen in others. It is true that if you observe an action of someone else, either positive or negative, your point of reference must be based on the fact that this trait is also within you or that you are familiar with the action because of self-knowledge about it. However, the trait or characteristic or action could also be a mirror to you of something that you have already overcome. Perhaps it is something you have found no longer useful for yourself in interactions with others, or for the attainment of your goals and ideals for self. In this way another individual could mirror or reflect to you your own growth. Not everyone reflects to you exactly where you are in the present moment of your growth. Try to discern the difference between a reflection that could signal you about something it would be best to overcome, something you have already experienced and overcome—which could help give you compassion for another's behavior—or, something that actually reflects or mirrors to you your potential.

As you go about your life, you may meet someone who is artistic, kind, brilliant—with any of these qualities and more. As you notice these qualities in others, you might ask yourself what your point of reference is for that observation. How is it that you do recognize these aspects of the character of others? Couldn't it be because these qualities also lie dormant within you as well? Interestingly, as in the life of Jesus of Nazareth, what was the point of reference for those who trusted their own feelings to know him as a Christ, beyond his words? Was it because those qualities were also latent within them, and . . . was his presence meant to encourage and reflect this? Could this have been a part of his message?

# The Religion Called "Becoming"

"BECOMING," a term often used  to describe a process associated with the spiritual quest, can become a preoccupation and, if prolonged, create a subtle diversion from the simplicity of "I am."

For some this is not unlike a new-age religion that can perpetuate separation from others who are not of like mind. However, this process of growth brought many people into a greater level of conscious awareness where they went beyond much of their previous confusion, dogma or beliefs. It is far wiser, however, to avoid getting caught up on *any* type of diversion from knowing self.

Conversely, in the acknowledgement of our free will, anyone can stay on a metaphysical wheel of "becoming" in order to "overcome self," but even the "journey of becoming" for many has been an arduous task and an over-empowered distraction from acknowledging in the present that self is already divine. The thought of being closer—rather than already there—creates a need for religion, doctrine and new age or other dogma, which perpetuates the mistaken notion that we need something outside of us to realize the God/Source within.

It is easy to embrace the piousness of a religion called, "I am a spiritual person; I go to church, synagogue, temples; I communicate with saints and other unseen masters, so I know more and therefore I am better than everyone else."

I've certainly experienced certain groups and organizations, where, the closer some people thought they were to God the further they got from the other people in their lives, because they judged them as being "less than" in being spiritual. It seems very true, as someone once said to me, "Whenever you join, you separate." Since then I've come to see the depths of knowledge within the eyes of a young child, life wisdoms in the face of the aged, and I have learned to cherish every individual's existence. . . . I know that very existence to be the ultimate in spiritual expression in and of itself. Therefore any "becoming" process, may temporarily make one feel better and "closer to God," but "closer" is still once removed in attitude from the awareness of and everyone's being in oneness.

Life crises can seem insurmountable without the spiritual inner strength of *personal* empowerment. Such crises can lead to a feeling of disillusionment with or abandonment by an exterior God, resulting for many in a rejection of faith in life. The attitude of *exterior* God alone often does not support the strength that comes from the awareness of the already *existent* inner God. From this awareness one can draw sustenance in order to receive nurturance and guidance.

A very positive and life affirming action is to

contemplate the inner essence of what we all are, and go directly to realizing this, thereby avoiding attitudes that say "We're not."

Make a very conscious effort to seek out the divinity of all things, and surround yourself with people who support and participate in a life-affirming, life-loving perspective. Surround yourself with that which brings you joy and with people who love you just because you breathe. Know that your very existence merits the love you seek. This restores you in life with unlimited and ultimate choices as I believe was originally intended for all.

It is far more the nature of the living of
Jesus of Nazareth than the words. Most
of us cannot remember the words. It is
how he lived that we remember; it is
how we live that matters

## Chapter Five

# The Second Coming: A Person . . . or an Attitude?

*Personal Christ / attuning to your ideal / think the best of yourself / it is how he lived / herald the consciousness of peace.*

CHRIST IS AN ATTITUDE WAITING WITHIN ALL to be birthed. Christ is an attitude through which all things can be seen anew.

This latent attitude may emerge at any time with an individual's desire and will. We have been conditioned in many cultures to function from the attitude of being "human" only. We have become informed, through biblical and cultural myths of what a Christ is supposed to be, and we are so aware of what we should be doing based on our limited information, that it is counter-productive to the natural flow and *acceptance of* our own individual Christ energy and attitude.

Many people in the West have an enslavement to the idea that only Jesus the Nazarene could become a Christ. As such the term *Christ* has also become a very heavy ideal and for some an intimidation; thus, the simplicity of it has seemingly been very difficult to embrace.

Realizing, living and reflecting to others that we are one with the Light and Supreme Thought equates a Christ—one who emanates and lives the knowledge of oneness with God in all things.

I believe that as long as anyone thinks of what Christhood was like for Jesus and does not include what it will be like for self, they will continually delay their own Christ expression. Others through our history have been born as babes and lived to become Christs. The similarities are evident, Buddha, Mohammed and Zoroaster to mention a few, yet they all had their own individual way. As such, each of our own paths is every bit as valid and holds the promise to be as significant as theirs. . . .

When we develop this profound overview we shall start to affect life rather than being an effect of it, for we can then have more dominion over our lives. This explains how the world may be in chaos, yet a master can still walk in joy . . . in possession of a deeper understanding and wisdom.

# Personal Christ

STORIES of Jesus depicted him as having performed magic, or miracles. This reminds me of the well-known story of the magical genie within Aladdin's enchanted lamp, which is not unlike the "magical" Christ power within self. Like the magical genie's power, the inner force of Christ enables us to accomplish far more than we dreamed possible. This power remains within the mysterious wonders of the mind, wherein waits latent genius, or the guardian spirit that, like the genie, remains to be released.

In recalling the story of Jesus's life, which depicts him going to the desert to contemplate, it seems more likely that Jesus contemplated what he knew he *was*, which brought him joy, and he focused on it, because he knew somewhere in that joy was God, the Father. He must have wanted to know that feeling and the power of that realization, to sustain it constantly . . . which certainly would have also released wonderful and magical powers— an example to all of us. As he said we are equally divine and need only evoke that in our understanding. It would be difficult to conceive that he went off into solitude to deeply contemplate that he was not divine. Accordingly, it does not matter what it seemingly appears to us or anyone else that we are not. That's only an illusion based on previous beliefs, and others measure it by what they feel *they're* not or what they've been told they weren't.

Christhood certainly would look a lot different in this, our century, than it did in those ancient times. I assume it is best not to compare. The life of Jesus, I believe, was never meant to be an intimidation; rather, it was meant to be  an example to encourage fellow humans to look deeply into life. Remember Jesus said, "I am your brother, and what I can do you can do and more." We should ask ourselves, "How are we going to express our Christ attitude and bring that to the world?" Seeking our own answers to this question would allow us to blossom and live our potential.  As previously stressed, whatever our thoughts are placed upon increases the potential for that to become manifest.

## Attuning to Your Ideal

AS NOTED in chapter 3, science now has information to validate a communication that occurs between the thought, the molecule and the atom . . . all of which supports the concept that thought has a profound effect on life. I feel that is the same as saying the "kingdom of heaven is within"—meaning within human consciousness. To quote the Buddha, we have nothing to acquire, only to realize. Therefore, we should ask ourselves if what we are doing and thinking *truly serves our ideal*—thereby attuning our awareness. For, if we keep our minds and thoughts filled with our ideal, if we remember that we are of the Source, here for the experience called life, then why should we not expand our consciousness to create the experience that is our ideal, engaging our full potential with joy? If we are not living our ideal, we must not be contemplating it enough. We would benefit greatly by filling our minds with thoughts that serve our God self.

# Think the Best of Yourself

THINK THE VERY BEST of yourself. Instead of imagining the worst that seemingly has happened or could happen and focusing on what you don't have in your life, practice intentionally contemplating and imagining what it would be like for you to experience your fulfillment and unclaimed abundance in life.

Regarding abundance, it is important to know that when you give, you receive more. Money, love and personal prosperity follow an abundant attitude; the abundant attitude is not meant to only come after money, love and prosperity are present.

For example,  you may have a thought of love or abundance. The person or persons who receive this through thought, now have more in their life. And you can have the same results in yours. You have more than you started with. A loving attitude and the nature of sharing or recycling these things nurtures your greater abundance. Such is the meaning of the whole concept of tithing, for a great feeling of abundance comes from feeling abundant enough to give.

It is also important to be willing to receive. Some have difficulty in allowing help or love or any other gift of generosity from others. It may help to know that in receiving you also give, for you offer another the opportunity to give to you, and vice-versa.

Anyone who has ever experienced the feelings of giving or receiving knows there was far more exchanged than food, clothing or money—there was a sense of faith or hope in the abundance of the universe as well as fellow man. Instead of saying, "I do not have enough money, I am always in debt," which only reinforces what you don't want, affirm more positively what you want. Restate, "I want and desire more money." The same applies to having conversation that focuses upon illness or lack of any kind, such as having no companion. Be aware of the power of the spoken word. Instead, say, "I am open to having a loving relationship." Focus your manifesting thought energy on what does bring you joy and be clear about your intentions and empower them.

Know you can change your life if you are experiencing one that is not of joy. You have the power and the will to change it. If you feel you need assistance, ask—pray or meditate . . . and always remember to deeply express your feelings of gratitude for the gifts of life.

We are as precious as we have been repeatedly told, and, through celebrating our differences and uniqueness our individuality becomes the chiseling of ourselves. As long as we continue to assume and to perpetuate the intimidation that the Christ is only out there somewhere outside of us, it's always going to remain out there in concept.

What we all need are examples of each other living as Christ conscious beings. We've heard of enough masters, saints and holy ones seen and unseen to know it is possible. It is for us to start coming forward now— mirroring that realization to one another. It is humans looking to humans to see the potential that is necessary, for the words of inspiration have all been spoken. . . .

# It is How He Lived

WHAT DOES IT MEAN to be a light unto the world?  Does it mean that you go out and teach everyone? Not necessarily. It means that through living your life in greater awareness, in looking to see the divine within all things, *there is a felt sense of divinity* which lifts your biological frequency so that you can facilitate the consciousness of divine thought longer. It means that your body begins to emanate a feeling and a glow, like the glow of the light body, or the halo of Jesus.  It means that your light,  your *enlightened* consciousness is reflected in everything you say, do, speak and touch, and therein you are a light unto the world.

This theme of living one's "light" in the world was touched upon in the previous chapter, where the research of Frank Barr, M.D., involving the molecule, melanin and its association with light were mentioned. It is interesting to speculate on how thought and light interplay with consciousness. Barr explains that melanin is made of neurotransmitters capable of converting light energy; in fact, it seems centrally involved in control of all physiological and psychological activity.[2] Since Barr's hypothesis proposes that the mind is associated with very delicate projections, like antenna, from the membrane of nucleic cells, which are so sensitive that they respond to a single photon of light, it is interesting to speculate what happens biologically and psychologically with the transfer of light through melanin when we facilitate expanded, or, as said above, "more unlimited, divine thought." The indication seems to be that the more we attune our conscious minds to a felt sense of the divine Source within all things the more we are able to facilitate more light in our bodies.

---

[2] Barr's research suggests that melanin and its nervous-system counterpart, neuromelanin, organize, self-organize and regulate a vast range of biological processes in the human body. For Barr's theory see *Medical Hypotheses* (11: 1-140)

Thus, because of his level of conscious awareness, it is probably far more the nature of the living of Jesus that most remember rather than the words. Most people cannot remember his exact words alone. *It is how he lived that is most remembered.* So, it is not so much the words alone that we need to remember . . . as it is how *we live* that we must master.

I feel it is very appropriate to share here a story of Jesus told by a very wise and learned sage. He also called Jesus by his Hebrew name *Yeshua* and said:

Yeshua indeed was all that your history has recorded him to be—gentle, loving . . . and emanating God essence . . . for he understood and spoke of the kingdom of heaven that was within, and he was filled with the desire to go upon his mission, from village to village, to let the people know of that which was within them as well. He did not explicitly call himself "the Christ". . . ; the people did, based on how they felt in his presence. He himself did not walk in and say, "I am Yeshua and I am the Christ."

He didn't speak of the greatness of that which *he* was so much as he spoke of the oneness of God which implied that greatness. He spoke of the peace and joy that he felt within his being. Also, he understood well that this would emanate out into his auric field and travel, often being felt, by those who were receptive, before he ever entered a region. The people could feel something. How did they feel it? What was their point of reference? . . . It was the same light within them as well that started to respond to the anticipation and acknowledgement through association with this Christ, Yeshua. By the time he arrived, with his unconditional love and the depth of knowing and wisdom within his eyes, his look and touch, the people were expectant.

Did he ever get angry? Was he ever confused? Did he have turmoil? But of course! You haven't lived until you've had the experience of knowing that others expect you to heal them or of feeling the energy building in a region that you are coming to, where you are heralded. So, often on the dirt roads or the dry, dusty cobblestones the people would scurry— "He's coming!" and their expectations would build. The expectation itself had begun the healing for many; yet, he hadn't even been there yet. How did they know to celebrate? From where did this energy come? . . . It was the people and their anticipation, they innately knew they could be well if they wanted it. It was their right. They knew that there was something more to life than what they could see. They loved that "something." They didn't know what it was, but they loved and sought after it. So when he arrived, the energy, which had been building began to peak, and as he would walk through . . . "Jesus! Jesus!" they would say.

Long had been his trek through these lands, and in the heat the perspiration of the body would run upon the long hair. The feet would be bare except for the hide that protected the foot, and the dust from the roads would accumulate and cake upon the body; yet, with anticipation the people awaited his arrival. And so one who could not see would reach out and grab hold of his rough robe, and then feel a hand upon his own, that of the one Jesus who loved him regardless —and lo, he could see. And the others wanted to say, "This man Jesus, he has given him vision!" Humbly Jesus would say, "No, it is that which I am, the "Father" within me that is within you also that does this thing!..." They did not want to hear that. It was frightening; yet, some could relate to a *man*; it was *he* doing the healing. They were sure of it... and it was that confusion that mystified them.

In yet another part of the village, on a quiet side road, on the outskirts, where there was no cobblestone, just the dirt and a bit of mud, all caked upon the village walls, there were those likened to lepers. They had heard also of this one who was called a Christed being and that he could bring forth a miraculous healing for them. They had suffered enough and long had been outcasts of the region in which they lived. They had much opportunity to contemplate life and its purpose, and they were ripe for belief in this one. The air became more electric with their anticipation of his arrival. They did not judge the grooming of his body and the bronzeness that occurred, which appeared to be leatherlike on his skin.

When he arrived in these places he often felt quite humble to see they awaited him. After all, he was just a man who understood many things. At this time he did not yet know this all preceded him. He would walk into this region having heard that the lepers often stayed at the outskirts, and he would often go there first, for he deemed them to be the most needy—and knew they were judged by others to be the least worthy. It was his will to gravitate toward them first, and as he arrived they would say, "Jesus, he is here." They would call out his name, and he would look. Their anticipation would build as they would look up into his eyes, and he, in turn, could love them no more than if it was himself who suffered. He would put his hand upon them, and often they would be healed. He would say, "This is not I alone who do this thing. It is the Father within us both—both." The leper would look upon his skin and then weep with joy and dance among the others.

Then came the conflict. What of the man who wasn't sure of this experience. He was not sure of this man Jesus, and he was ill, but his daughter who greatly loved her father would say, "Father, he is coming to our village! He is the Christed one. Come! We have heard of him. He will heal you!"

The father would answer "I do not know, daughter, if I believe in this man. He might be blasphemous." And the daughter would say, "But, Father, I fear greatly that you shall not live, and I love you dearly. Pray tell, Father, won't you come with me to greet him?" and she would scurry her father to come, and he would, for she was known to have a temper, and when Jesus would come by she would say, "Jesus, Jesus, my father, heal my father!" And Yeshua would look at this man who would not meet him in the eye, for the man did not feel convinced of who he was and feared it would show in his eyes. Then Yeshua would say, "I cannot, daughter, heal your father. Love him for that which he is. Judge him not."

The daughter persisted, "But why?" she replied, and the father reluctantly would concede, "Alright," and he would allow the embrace of this man Yeshua, but the father would not be healed. The daughter was perplexed and tears would well up and run down her face, for she saw her father appeared to be the same. Yeshua would go upon his way, and as night time fell, and as he sat out upon a ridge, some of the people followed hoping to dialogue with him. Quiet was his mood and pensive, for, you see, many gave to him responsibilities that were not his alone and these were heavy upon his being. For they thought, "Why is it that he would heal one, but he would not heal another?" And he would say, "It is not I alone. It is the God within us both, the Father within us both that does this thing." But they could not understand that. They felt it had to be the man. They saw that, and they thought therefore it was the man who did this thing. Yet, it was the consciousness exchange that played the role, that healed or not. Either they engaged with a loving presence, and *together* would bring forth a healing, or deny it, regardless. Because all *are that powerful in thought!*

Often many misunderstandings arose and burdens were placed upon him. Some would say that it must be magic that he does, and often, in simplicity, he would repeat, "It is not I alone that does this thing, but the spirit that dwells within ye. That which I can do ye can do, and greater things, for indeed I am your brother."

It has not changed to this day. So it is probable that Jesus had moments of feeling it was difficult at times to live in this world as a Christ, for many wanted to give him their power . . . so, if you feel frustrated from time to time, do not assume frustration cannot be within the realm of facilitating Christ consciousness within you. Because so many in another time could not accept what he taught—that, "I am your brother, what I can do you can do"—does not mean it is the same today.

Jesus was born a babe. So were we all. He *became* a Christ. We as well are all Christs latent within us. It is not so much that as you become a Christ the world changes—rather your perception of it does; thereafter, with grace and ease, what your life brings to you in joyous fulfillment and inner peace is vastly exalting of the life experience! As John said in the Book of Revelations, "I saw a new heaven and a new earth."[3] I see one too, only it looks like heaven and peace on earth coming from a unified, or Christ-like consciousness.

There are celebrations, changes and new challenges in many places in the world today. These changes began first in the minds and hearts of people all over the world, who first sought, and are now creating, alternative approaches and solutions. So far this emerging consciousness sounds more like the roar of student's voices as they call out for freedom in Tiananmen Square, China; it sounds like the crumbling of the Berlin wall and reform in Eastern Europe; it sounds like the words

---

[3] 21:1

*glasnost* and *perestroika* in Russia and the intertwining economy of a global world. It looks like the unifying of people worldwide as food and other aid from one nation is shipped to those in need in another. It feels like the joy in the long-suffering hearts that are now reunited with loved ones as nations unite for peace, and, seen or unseen, the walls that separate people come down. It will also feel for some like the expectation of life and opportunities yet to be explored and experienced. Some may and yet others may not have personally crossed the wall, brought the aid or called for freedom, but their thoughts were there because of their belief in the rights of freedom and happiness. We contributed to that emerging consciousness, and whenever one human spirit is set free we are all affected.

THE SECOND COMING of Christ has been prophesied, and I believe that it is indeed a truth. Though it is a truth of varied and greater meaning than often understood. It is a return inclusive of the embracing by the whole of humanity of the consciousness known in the West as Christ. It is not a solely separate event that takes place only outside of humanity. I do not think the Christ shall return to be a savior, but shall return instead to a people and a time, which shall both see and acknowledge him in equality as the brother he described himself to be. It shall be a capstone, if you will, to the understanding and the fruition of heaven and peace upon our earth, resulting from the acknowledgement of the God within all.

Herald the consciousness of peace!

There is no beginning and no ending to
the vast Source known as God

*Inconceivable as it seems to ordinary reason, you—and all other conscious beings as such—are all in all.  Hence this life of yours which you are living is not merely a piece of the entire existence, but is in a certain sense the* whole.
                    —*Physicist Erwin Schroedinger,*
                              My View of the World


# Chapter Six

---

# Oneness

*All are one / understanding interconnectedness and reincarnation / memory and consciousness / evolving beliefs / gestalt energy—the whole and its parts / multidimensional time / awareness of interconnections / contributing to life / effects of thought alignment / uniqueness is retained*

By NOW IT HAS BEEN FAIRLY WELL ESTABLISHED that "God" is neither a bearded entity who sits upon a cloud nor solely some exterior Source that determines individual destiny. Instead, this grand Source is, in fact, in oneness with us as well as all existence. . . .

As J. Krishnamurti has said in *First and Last Freedom:* "[T]he experiencer and the thing experienced are one. That integration [in consciousness] is necessary and has to be radically faced."

---

Also, as noted in the Gospel of John 17:21: "That they all may be One; as thou, Father, art in me, and I in thee, that they also may be One in us." The center of this theme of being "One" in consciousness is referred to as the Source consciousness, or the means by which we all are interconnected. Our origin from this Source supports us in the life experience we desire. . . . As said in the previous chapter, our power to live a joyous and fulfilled life— although it has always existed— seemingly increases in relation to our increased knowledge of the power of the universal creative Source that is also within us.

# All are One

THE EXTENT TO WHICH ONE DEVELOPS the abililty to intuitively access more expanded realms of knowledge correlates with the degree to which an individual experiences greater conscious awareness, or a sense of connection to all. It thus often includes a felt sense of unity, wholeness, or oneness with all things. All endeavors in which a consciously aware individual then participates reflect this emerging understanding of cosmic, or Christ consciousness, which includes but transcends the exclusive boundaries previously set on this concept *by any one religious interpretation.* As one writer so well said in the *Upanishads (Katha)* of ancient India:

> As the wind, though one, takes on new forms in
> whatever it enters; the Spirit, though One, takes new

forms in whatever that lives. He is within all, and is also outside. . . . There is one Ruler, the Spirit that is in all things, who transforms His one form into many. . . . [T]he wise who see Him in their souls attain the joy eternal. [1]

Attuning to this consciousness is how the "parts" of the Whole begin to realize and experience their wholeness through each other.

The realization of interconnection through consciousness can result in a more harmonious experience of life for all species. Individuals who have attained such an enlightened state of oneness are more conscious of their actions so that these actions are inclusive of the good of all. They innately know that when they assist and support the God/Source within another, therein they, too, are in benefit of this action. I feel Albert Einstein knew of what he spoke when he said:

> We all feel that it is indeed very reasonable and important to ask ourselves how we should try to conduct our lives. The answer is, in my opinion . . . achievement of harmony and beauty in the human relationships. It is undeniable that the enlightened Greeks and the old oriental sages had achieved a higher level in this all-important field.[2]

---

[1] See footnote 1 in ch. 1.

[2] *The Human Side*, Selected and Edited by Helen Dukas and Banesh Hoffman (Princeton University Press, 1981)

# Understanding
# Interconnectedness and Reincarnation

IT IS APPROPRIATE IN THE RETHINKING of many common and accepted beliefs to discuss reincarnation to see how, if at all, it applies within the concept of oneness. Many, and the number is exponentially growing in the West, may have at some time acknowledged the reality of reincarnational selves. Embracing the philosophy of reincarnation assisted us to better understand ourselves, families, friends and all those who co-inhabit this planet with us.

Along with the emerging understanding of the universe as a constant existence, an evolved concept of reincarnation must ultimately also go beyond the boundaries of linear time and include simultaneous time. Found within the concept of reincarnation, where it is believed that the human spirit evolves through linear time to greater levels of awareness, is an assumption that all incarnations are finished except for the life being actually lived at this present moment. This belief is a natural outcome of the worldview that time flows neatly from past to future.

This linear "flow" is a relative truth that assists us in understanding our world; however, now that science acknowledges "time" as a human creation, reincarnation can be taken into a new framework that includes parallel, or simultaneous time.[3] Scientists now postulate a parallel universe phenomenon wherein time can be seen as going either from the past to the future, or from the future toward the past. In this hypothesis there is speculation that a precognitive or déja vu event actually happens in a future time and is viewed from the so-called "past" because our brains have the capacity to tap into both worlds simultaneously.[4]

## Memory and Consciousness

ALL INFORMATION, past, present or future resides in the constant reservoir of consciousness, which is why it is always accessible.[5] Biochemist Rupert Sheldrake explores

---

[3] See *Space, Time and Beyond,* by Fred Alan Wolf (Bantam, 1982) and *Parallel Universes* (Simon and Schuster, 1988) as well as *J'ai vecu quinze milliards d'annees* (I have lived 15 billion years) by physicist Jean Charon (Albin Michel, publisher).

[4] For a wonderful novelistic treatment, see *The Education of Oversoul Seven* trilogy by Jane Roberts (Pocket Books, 1976).

[5] See the work of biologist Rupert Sheldrake and his theory of formative causation, i.e., a morphogenetic field, or form generating field exists that is drawn upon or fed into by all information in the universe, e.g., human thought. Sheldrake: *A New Science of Life* and *The Presence of the Past.* (New York: Times Books, 1988).

the idea that memory is a quality of nature. He questions that there are eternal and immutable laws of nature and proposes that living organisms are affected by the past of similar living organisms through morphic resonance. He suggests there may be morphic, biodynamic and electromagnetic fields of all systems, such as living organisms, animals, humans that can be seen as containing a memory, and that this memory can be affected by (that is, given input by) us, and that any of this input can be accessed by us through the phenomenon of morphic resonance. All information would thus become available to us through our brain/mind connection with this morphogenetic (lit.: form generating) field.

It is interesting to note the correlation here with psychologist Carl Jung's theories about the Collective Unconscious, which many respectful critics have pointed out isn't really unconsciousness, but rather a continuous, collective and active consciousness at a deeper level of awareness. From this reservoir of deep consciousness come symbols and ideas found in dreams, prayer and meditation. The evident corollary is that all information, all knowledge exists within a field of consciousness that is shared by the collective.

# Evolving Beliefs

THESE EMERGING understandings we are discussing have

always been present. The only thing that really changes is our ability to perceive them. This is true of any understandings we have perceived, for example, there are beliefs we have needed to discard or replace from childhood to the present day.

An historical example arises with previous ideas about slavery. Changes were made because some people did not feel good about slavery, and some of them realized their feelings concerned their own issues of freedom. Eventually freedom became more the norm in our society. We all became beneficiaries of this freedom, for a race that was seen as a slave race is now one that adds to the cultural enrichment of an entire world of people. Another example refers to an earlier time when someone would say the word *Japanese*, and Americans would associate it with war, anger and lost loved ones. Now we think of cars, technology, sushi bars and an ancient culture of acknowledged richness.

We are evolving as a global society, reevaluating our beliefs toward one another, the planet and what is called God. While evaluation is always wise and should be encouraged, it is important that none of us feel threatened or fearful of loss in the overwhelmingness of what is perceived to be greater information. Any time we feel we may lose our individual invested beliefs or identity, we may feel driven to do battle to maintain them within our present framework or belief . . . but that would be to deny our identity its chance to expand and grow.

As Herbert Spencer said, "There is a principle . . . which cannot fail to keep a man in everlasting ignorance; that principle is contempt, prior to investigation."

# Gestalt Energy—The Whole and its Parts

THE EMERGING PERCEPTION of God is that this Source is more of a gestalt, or integrated whole with characteristics that are more than the summation of all of its parts.

As in the hologram, where in no matter how many pieces a unit is separated, each piece contains within it the graphic image of the whole, we create more parts of the whole.[6] This gestalt energy is a creative, ever-expanding energy of profound love and supreme intelligence that supports us in life, and it is not restricted to the structure of time and space.

Let's explore this concept and how it applies to you and me. Using the analogy of a water-filled balloon, with the water representing the gestalt Source, imagine a

---

[6] A hologram is a graphic image resulting from the use of laser light imaging and the recreation of interference patterns. The result is that if a glass image is broken into a thousand pieces, each of the pieces will depict the same image that was originally seen in the entire glass plate.

multitude of holes in the balloon and water streaming out continually from each individual hole. All streams, each representing an individual person, are connected through the water within the balloon (representing the Source). [SEE FIG. 6]

Further, imagine that as the water seeps out of the separate holes—an analogy for the unique and individual human adventure with all its variations of race, color, religious preference and cultural environment—it travels in many different frequencies. These are not greater or lesser, just different and unique frequencies. Each expresses as an individual life, whether in the 1200s, 1700s, or B.C.; it doesn't matter what the time frame is.

# Multidimensional Time

THESE VARIOUS LIVES may not necessarily be linear; they could possibly be simultaneous. Linear time is only a purposeful framework we have created in order to support us in our physical world. We have subsequently and conveniently fit reincarnation into that structure.

As noted above, many researchers are altering the structure of belief to include the concept of simultaneity of time. Much awareness seems to be unfolding at this time as a needed balance between our advanced intellect and less developed spiritual and intuitional development

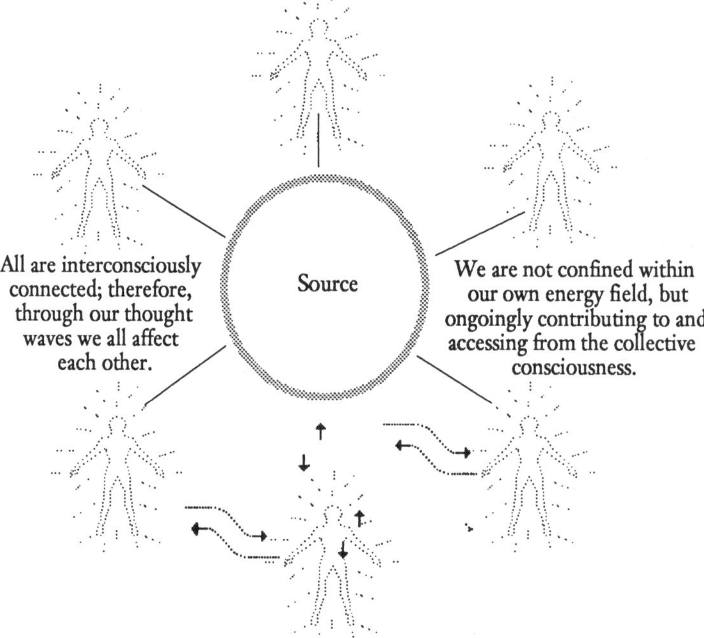

Varied and unique individual
personality selves expressing the God
Source in physical form...

Source

All are interconsciously
connected; therefore,
through our thought
waves we all affect
each other.

We are not confined within
our own energy field, but
ongoingly contributing to and
accessing from the collective
consciousness.

Each of us are purposeful, cherished, uniquely
honored and loved human beings.

Every individual is in contact with the implicate order, with
all that is around us. —physicist David Bohm *

*From an interview with Renee Weber, *Revision*, Fall 1978

**Fig. 6**

takes place. Many are beginning to realize their oneness with the God/Source and with one another, and to know the power of that which has always been available for us. In addition, within this awareness our perception of ourselves is beginning to transcend linear time as an absolute structure. This topic will be expanded in later chapters.

Throughout human history there have been those noted ones such as St. John, Meister Eckhart, Hildegard of Bingen, Krishnamurti, not to mention Jesus and Buddha, who have gained greater awareness from an exploration of their divine origin. They simply began by asking "Who am I?" This question led them inward into the exploration of self as the "I."

They expanded their perception of "I" and gained the awareness that they were also an aspect or part of the "whole," and that this was simultaneously the personality self as well. "I" at a certain level of awareness becomes the "I" that exists in all—the not-separate "I."

They then further realized there is a connectedness, which, when explored, ultimately leads to the realization that others can experience a similar connection. Thus, when individuals seek their origin, they ultimately discover its dwelling within themselves as well as in others and in all else. Once they realize their connection with the God/Source they begin to wonder about their relationship with the rest of humanity.

Because we all come from the same Source, we are in a sense aspects of one another. That does not, however, detract from the uniqueness of our own expression and the fact that we are the creators of our own reality—each of us purposeful, cherished and uniquely honored and loved human beings. . . . We are never separate from the conscious "whole." Because we live, we make a difference. That is why it is impeccable to think thoughts and do actions that support the development of the full potential of our race.

The ideal of loving all of humanity can only follow when you have exercised love within yourself first. The ideal must first be understood, embraced and allowed within ourselves. It is difficult to see the God/Source in someone else if you have not first seen It within your own being. To be comfortable with the variedness and differences of others, it is important not to negate these very uniquenesses and differences in oneself. Avoid conforming self to a mold of sameness, or to a structure of mediocrity. Instead, by allowing and supporting the varieties of expression in others, you simultaneously do the same for self. . . freeing your own spirit self for unlimited expression.

## Awareness of Interconnections

IN BROADENING OUR PERCEPTIONS of ourselves and each other, we become more loving, compassionate and closer in our understandings of all those around us. The perceived separateness and differences we previously held are *no longer* seen as threats or aggravations, but rather as varied, individualized, personal expressions of our shared Source. In actuality, these are truly differences to be celebrated, for all people are expressing and acting out individual and personal choice. . . .

As our perspectives broaden, resulting from greater awareness, we often recognize this awareness in others of like mind, and together we intentionally participate in the conscious support of the "whole" that all of us are expressing and experiencing in life. Therein we gradually add to a more loving shift in mass consciousness to the concern for and support of all. Some may call this the Hundredth Monkey concept, or another could say it is an increased attunement to universal or collective group consciousness.

# Contributing to Life

ONE WAY THIS SHIFT IN CONSCIOUSNESS seems to work is that the thought frequency resulting from the acknowledgement of oneness . . . emits from our auric, bioelectric field with a conscious expression of support for the potential within all. Then simultaneously, the coveted Christ understanding is implemented in life. Ultimately the message of over two thousand years becomes realized and lived, for you begin to experience all as aspects of God, and you perceive everyone as interrelated.

*Each of us is accountable for our own life contribution.* Through living life with joy we each contribute more joy to the whole of life. Therein, when someone else desires assistance or guidance, our own experiences help assist them vibrationally through the energy of the collective conscious mind with anything we have realized. A purposeful affirmation is, "I am joy and fulfillment, and I acknowledge this as my divine right in this physical expression." Thoughts are that powerful!

Any suffering, hate, joy, love, healing—any emotion, any experience is felt throughout the Whole. This is then added to or drawn from according to an individual's intent and preferences in the life experience. As discussed, what we think and feel resonates to the whole of the Source that is all . . . , and that communication is held there within the Source for all of us to access. [SEE FIG. 6]

## Effects of Thought Alignment

THOUGHTS OF LOVE and joy are referred to as high frequency, divine thoughts. By taking dominion over our own emotions and thoughts, and by expanding our belief in oneness, we ensure through this belief that we are worthy to experience love, joy and peace here and now. As stated previously, thoughts have a profound and rippling effect on our own self-esteem and psyche, as well as the impressions sent to another. It is easy to determine this for yourself.

If you observe yourself express something that is less worthy or out of alignment with what you want, say masterfully and lovingly what you *do* want and mean and simply send love and blessings to follow. Complete your thought or sentence with an additional one that supports the potential you know exists for you. You might find yourself saying someone is a pain in the neck. You can rephrase that sentence and say, "This person is a challenge for me, but I look forward to seeing change, and I would like to see him do such and such. We could then have a relationship that is happier." Say this to your employer, mate, friends. Don't end with an incomplete negative sentence, but finish your sentences with what you want to happen. This empowers the positive end results you truly seek to have occur for yourself.

You might feel irritated because someone may mirror to you a past characteristic or trait of yourself that caused you to suffer once. You may not enjoy the attitude that particular person expresses, but you can still *love* the God/ Source that is within that one and thus be impeccable as well as in alignment with the Source of which you both are. Perhaps this is why it has always been said that love is so supreme.

As you realize and  perceive the aspect of self that is divine in someone else, you will also support them in the divinity of their own identity.  Inner awareness results in cosmic awareness. As a result of all people recognizing and feeling themselves to be God expressing in form, what emerges is greater fulfillment of human potential, *and the outcome is an expanded and enhanced experience of life for all.*

Not only does this happen in physical evolution of the human species alone, but it also occurs in the evolution in our awareness of consciousness. As seen in Figure 7, as individuals become aware of their true nature and consciousness, they recoginze their source in and interface with the Divine Consciousness, which by that fact now includes them in greater awareness and in that sense is Itself expanded.

# Uniqueness is Retained

TO REITERATE, THE DEGREE to which we perceive ourselves as isolated individuals existing separately from the Source and each other, is how much we experience the limitation and confusion within that framework. It is embattlement between the parts, each of us, that causes the consciousness of fragmentation. The collective reality we co-create is in effect of  the degree to which we begin to see self in the "Wholeness" of the God/Source. The

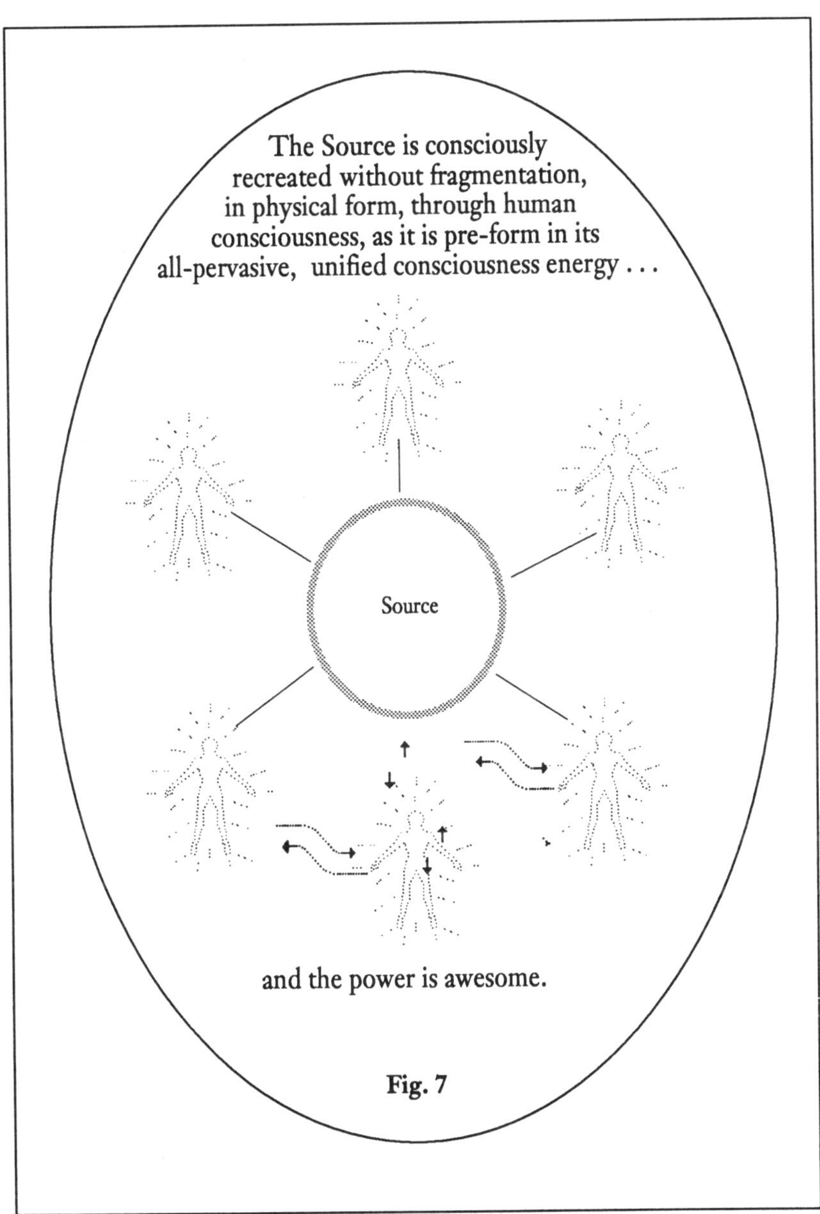

The Source is consciously
recreated without fragmentation,
in physical form, through human
consciousness, as it is pre-form in its
all-pervasive,  unified consciousness energy . . .
Source
and the power is awesome.

**Fig. 7**

more we see our oneness with all things, the more enhanced is our own individual expression as "self." Identification with "all that is"—oneness—does not threaten, dilute nor negate "self" as an individual personality expressing uniquely as "I am." It clarifies and strengthens it!

Each person's life experience is still unique and equally valid through individual interpretation. Each person always retains free will and choice, and ongoingly has access to the cumulative information from their unique life experience, which has simultaneously been contributed to the Whole. *In addition, each person also has the experiences of all others to draw upon.*

Through our very existence we have a profound effect on all of reality. . . . We co-create through our collective consciousness. The Source expresses out to the many "parts"—or aspects—or individual selves. *When each of us begins to acknowledge and love internally the Source within us, we begin to acknowledge and love this same Source within each other, and the whole is lovingly recreated, without fragmentation, in our shared reality of life.*

To damn another, to harm another, therefore, would not be supportive of ourselves, much less of the others. Regardless of how repulsed people can be by those who have done a horrendous crime against another, somewhere, within that criminal is still the same God/Source . . . . *To condemn another is, at some level, to condemn self.* So it is said to "love another as thyself." It can be enlightening to observe and then discern what another may be going through; what created their hate or sorrow? Few crimes are committed by those who feel genuinely loved.

There is no beginning and no ending to the vast Source known as God. One has to conclude, therefore, that the most central focus of all that is must be found within one's own self. This is especially apparent, and the unified energy field commonly shared by all is enhanced when one is focused in cosmic conscious awareness.

All are interconsciously connected;
therefore, through our thought waves
we all affect each other

*Physicists have come to see that all their theories of natural phenomena, including the laws they describe, are creations of the human mind. . . . The physicist begins his inquiry into the essential nature of things by studying the material world. Penetrating even deeper realms of matter, he has become aware of the essential unity of all things and events. More than that, he has also learned that he himself, and his consciousness, are an integral part of this unity.*
—*Fritjof Capra*, The Tao of Physics

## Chapter Seven

# Universal Mind: Exploring Interconscious Connectedness

*Healing with mind / positive codependency / discoveries, supportive thoughts and osmosis / the collective parts / beliefs and unlimited creativity / beliefs / unified consciousness and families of thought / thoughts and attraction / Idols, celebrities and prodigies*

IT WOULD TAKE some naiveté to live in this century, in a modern civilization, and miss the fact that there is much concern for the life and wellness of Earth in regard to pollutants, ecology, natural resources etc. Could it be, however, the greatest pollution that encompasses our planet is from negative and unconstructive thoughts and attitudes?

We as a race must begin to understand ever more the impact we have on our planet through our consciousness. It is interesting to speculate what positive effect it shall have upon our planet as humanity ultimately recognizes the vastness of our interconscious connection and our collective influence on the environment.

As stated earlier, scientific researchers are recognizing that the human body emits an auric field which functions much like a transmitter and a receiver of thought energy, and in this way we have an influence through our thought and attitudes upon all life around us, including the animal and plant kingdoms. Peter Tompkins and others have done some fascinating experiments to prove that our very thoughts affect plants.[1] The Native American tradition provides fine examples of a respect for and alliance with the plant and animal kingdoms.

# Healing with Mind

I BELIEVE that our planet is a receptor for our thoughts,

---

[1] Tompkins, *The Secret Life of Plants* (Harper & Row, 1984)

and just as the medical field acknowledges more and more that malaligned thoughts and attitudes are precursors to ailments and diseases in the human body, so the earth is affected by our thought and attitudes. Therefore, as we heal the mind and emotions of man, not only will the body heal, but the whole of the planet will also surely follow. This healing of the planet is affected by our consciousness as we become more aligned with an expanded global awareness. When we emit thoughts that reflect a deep love and support for all of life, wherever we are, our planet receives the effects of these powerful thought frequencies.

I think it is very appropriate here, with the concern for the animals and environment that is evident today, to draw attention to how our thoughts affect them. I would like to quote a few of my favorite lines from the poetry of James Allen in his small, classic piece, *As a Man Thinketh*.

> Mind is the Master-power that moulds and makes,
> And Man is Mind, and evermore he takes
> The tool of Thought, and, shaping what he wills,
> Brings forth a thousand joys, a thousand ills:—
> He thinks in secret, and it comes to pass
> Environment is but his looking-glass.

We, through our collectively shared Source, are supreme beings, and we share with one another the power to co-create an improved existence in life based on our beliefs and desires. Thus, it would serve us well to believe in, desire and intentionally contemplate the better world we all want.

# Positive Codependency, Animals and Nature

"CODEPENDENCY" is today understood to imply dysfunction and destructive dependency. Actually, it can be (and is) a beautiful, positive and natural way of relating between animals, nature and man. In so far as the term is negative, it must be understood that negative implications are not the whole story. There is need for a more balanced and insightful understanding of codependency.

For example, the worldwide ramifications of the destruction of even one portion of the rainforest is seen in our current awareness as being detrimental to all species on earth. It may start as harming only the insects and animals of a given area, but it ripples out to harm the whole earth ecosystem.

Among the concerns for a kinder world today are those for the rare and endangered species as well as for domestic animals. Although animals have their own will and instinct that govern them, their world obviously is also affected by the will of humans.

At first this may seem an unfair notion. When, however, more people realize and acknowledge that animals are of the same Source as us, more will honor them as such.

Therefore, when we capture and bring an animal from the wild into captivity, we then have taken—and should accept—responsibility to challenge ourselves within our race to extend our intuitiveness into interspecies communications so as to understand each unique animal of this whole kingdom and not usurp or negate their rights and will, establishing a needed balance. Bringing animals out of their intended homes is a practice I fondly hope will soon be replaced with a means by which we can all observe them in their own natural habitats.

Animals are not to be enslaved or abused, but rightfully to be treasured by us in our oneness. Therein they experience a human world where they are all safe and cherished within the free will of an enlightened humanity.

I'm convinced that our race will ultimately form co-existence in peace when all people understand that we are—through consciousness—interconnected regardless of which culture, political system or region of the world is ours.

With the quantum shift in consciousness taking place within humanity, and in an understanding of conscious interconnection—which knowledge itself results in a nurturing disposition toward all of life—it is very appropriate to anticipate that we will soon fully see and experience again the true marvel and beauty of each other, of how our forests can increase and thrive, the skies become clearer, water purer, and wildlife more abundant.

Being part of the world's life system as a human is both a privilege and a responsibility.

# Discoveries, Supportive Thoughts and Osmosis

ONE INTERESTING WAY to view discoveries, for example, the discovery of penicillin or a new galaxy, is from the perspective that it has always been there—thus the term *dis-covered*. This is to say that what has been discovered has always existed, but, when many people—including those who believe in unobvious and uncommon solutions—emit a desire through thought frequency for an alternative energy, medicine or deeper view of the cosmos, the conscious connection helps to "lift the veil" of prejudice or ignorance toward this discovery and new knowledge and realizations. This shift, or "openness" of attitude allows insights into what was always possible. The possibility is then accessed and at times scientifically formulated, and this then may be termed a *modern discovery*.

It seems when people do more than just believe in the unobvious and the uncommon solution, but they also intentionally desire that it come forth, the desire creates, through consciousness, a vortex of energy supportive of the discovery. For instance, when a scientist is in a lab with his or her focus, knowledge, experience and a desire for answers, oftentimes the supportive thought energies of others, as part of the whole mind field, assist in drawing in knowledge electromagnetically (or, as some have put it, the answers "fall out of the thin air" into one's lap as luck, coincidence, destiny or synchronicity—all of which are the outcome of desire and focused intent). Could it be that the right things work because they are supported by the energies of one person or a collective of people who believed in greater possibilities prior to their "discovery"? Could it be that these people thereby assisted, or even created the probability that the new discovery would be "found?"

Of course this could apply to advancement in any field. This is working around the world in wondrous ways. It is working so well that it has penetrated not only science and medicine, but also politics.

Just one example is that the Berlin Wall has come down. It has been in the process of coming down since it went up. The aspirations and the desire and the will of people brought it down. Ultimately, over time, all contributed to that. You may have desired this. You may not have been there. You may not have walked through it as you, but an aspect of you walked through it—a bit of your consciousness. Many are now in freedom, because you and many others called out and would have nothing less than that understanding of freedom, and your will contributed to the consciousness that influenced others to move through it.

# The Collective Parts

THERE is currently a greater consciousness emerging in the world that wants to cooperate in the support of the collective. Some refer to this as a new age of consciousness, or even simply a new age. An interesting example of this arises in the great hope for fusion energy, which has been awaited for a long time. The word *fusion* means uniting together, or blending. The hope for it could be seen also as symbolizing a hoped for unification resulting from an expansion of awareness in humankind of our shared Source and its many faceted expressions for the benefit of the "whole"; all the parts unite and work together. If we, as a seemingly singular self, choose to be supported by something that in any way has a detrimental effect on others or the planet, therein lies a hidden duality that contradicts the consciousness of oneness. Ultimately, it isn't even for our own "singular" benefit, for it is not harmonious to the spirit of oneness.

Tomorrows are co-created, through the interplay of consciousnesses, which consists of the thoughts and intentionality of all members of humanity.

A consciousness that is being encouraged, though it has always allowed for individual prosperity, is a consciousness that is accompanied by a deeper awareness of its effect. Prosperity that accompanies this awareness always endures. This means it has an effect that is non-detrimental and non-conflicting with all other levels of existence because it is supportive of all life. Thus, within the divine Source the consciousness of prosperity is accepted as benefitting the whole as it does so for any one self. The life Source-energy is unbounded, unrestricted, pure, and It is divine.

## Beliefs and Unlimited Creativity

ALL THINGS STEM first from thought and consciousness. Everything, therefore, ever done, ever learned, invented or created still exists in the whole of collective thought consciousness, or the Universal Mind, for any of us to access.[2]

We can access that information with or without structured rules, degrees, certificates or official doctrines, for all information originates from the universal Mind— therefore, there are many ways to learn and create. An example of this is seen in Walter Russell. He left school at the age of ten in order to help his family. He put himself through art school at the age of fifteen but had no other

---

[2] Note the previous chapter footnotes to Biologist Rupert Sheldrake's theory of the M-field and his *The Presence of the Past.*

formal schooling. He became a very successful painter, architect, sculptor, writer and businessman, and numbered among his friends Theodore Roosevelt. He received acclaim from other world leaders such as King Albert of Belgium, Thomas Edison, Rudyard Kipling and hundreds of other authors, scientists, statesmen and geniuses in all the arts. His many accomplishments in most areas came without formal training, and when asked how he was able to do so much he explained that all information exists in the universal mind for anyone to tap.[3] He simply made up his mind that he was going to do something, and was not deterred if there did not seem to be an immediate or clear way for the thing to be done. He envisioned himself doing the job and through his very intent was able to acheive all he did. He felt he accessed the information he needed from the Universal/Divine Mind.

To access knowledge that you do not have, desire, contemplate and focus on what you want. Think of your brain as being an instrument, and, just as you would tune into the frequency of a radio station on your radio receiver, or as you would aim your satellite dish for television reception, focus your mind on what you wish to know. This act will assist you to find what you want in the Source of the universal Mind. As Plato said, "This kind of

---

[3]Russell lived a fascinating life, as depicted in the biography *The Man Who Tapped the Secrets of the Universe* by Glenn Clark (MacAlester Park Publishing Co., 21st ed., 1988 ).

knowledge is a thing that comes in a moment like a light kindled from a leaping spark which, once it has reached the soul, finds its own fuel." As explained earlier, once you access the idea, your own individual creative energy will carry you through to a creative act. This manner of accessing knowledge is similar to the process of osmosis, for all knowledge is within the collective whole and can therefore be accessed at any time.

This can also be recognized as that undercurrent of energy that draws people of like mind or intent together, for instance, with a group of artists who are drawn to one city, such as Paris. The same is true when within a city certain colonies of musicians, business groups or religious congregations subtly resonate to one another and form collectives of supportive consciousness. This does not mean that you need to be physically present in such a group to access the wisdom, the excellence or the genius. The gathering of knowledge in this way is commonly experienced as intuitive insight, or inspiration.

When you understand how intuition can be accessed and used, you can more *deliberately* engage and sustain creative urges; thereby, you can go beyond the precedent of the often frustrating and random spurts of intuition and creativity you may have become used to experiencing. An important note arises here:  From this perspective there is no need to use competition or scarcity as a motivation to create anything, for *creativity is seen to derive from a universally abundant and perpetual Source!*

# Beliefs

IF SOMEONE tells you about a dream that they want to bring into fruition, and you say to them "You can't do that, you have no schooling or experience in this," then you limit your own dreams and future to those same rules. If you empower such a belief, then you allow it. You may not let yourself succeed because you believe in those rules. Once you've set them up for someone else, the rules then also apply to you. Therefore, to support someone else's fulfillment of their dreams is also to support and expect fulfillment of your own. Your beliefs create or negate the many options always available in this unlimited universe. Often certain beliefs can overstructure and thereby limit creativity. Deny yourself nothing—*believe in everything and choose with discernment* whatever you want as a life experience.

For instance, when you have a desire that a dream or ideal come true in your life, but believe that a certain circumstance need occur prior to the fulfillment of that dream, you then empower that rule or event to precede your dream fulfillment. The precedents you thought needed to happen (based on a preconditioned belief) may not need to occur at all for your dream or project to come into reality.

If not already familiar with them, you may choose to read the many biographies of noted people who have accomplished remarkable states of creative achievement, such as those about Thomas Edison, Abraham Lincoln, Eleanor Roosevelt, Walter Russell, etc., none of whom followed the formal and societal rules about "how it should be done"; that is to say, neither Edison nor Russell had degrees or certificates from formal institutes, yet each excelled in various endeavors.

Again, if you contemplate what you ask for, but believe there must be certain circumstances before you can receive it, then you empower those circumstances to precede it. Your will and intent are always universally supported.

*Choice is our responsibility and in it is our freedom.*

# Unified Consciousness
# and Families of Thought

WHEN THE "parts" begin to recognize the Source within their own personality self—an "I am" perspective—and extend this awareness to include others, what subsequently occurs is that the *whole* is recognized by its individual aspects. What follows is a more supportive unified consciousness in *physical expression*. The Source, as it has been expressed by most of us in our limited understanding and expression, is freed to its full potential as expressed through humankind. In this expression, the Source is no longer stuck or limited within a certain framework of belief, as many have held it. Of course, the Source *never was* limited, except in our perceptions of it.

From a broadened perspective, one sees that there is more wisdom, more compassion, wellness, greater abundance, and more deeply fulfilling relationships, all adding to a more meaningful life. It is interesting to note that someone who has not yet begun to explore these topics, and who may even challenge you and your beliefs, may through the process of resonance or osmosis be affected at a certain level of consciousness *because of your "enlightenment"* as well as that of others. Thus, another's quest for understanding of God can be stimulated by an osmosis-like effect from your own self, not to mention from the enlightened masters who have preceded us.

# Thoughts and Attraction

AN IMPORTANT POINT that bears repeating is that the thought/emotion vibrations electromagnetically emit from human consciousness. Our thoughts broadcast like unseen radio transmissions and are picked up and felt because we are electromagnetic beings. We can thus begin to attract individuals and thoughts of a parallel frequency that are supportive of our desired expression of personal creativity here in our lives at anytime we wish.

Thus people with similar "frequencies" and intent are drawn together to participate in common pursuits. In so doing they create a self-determined "family of thought." The people within these families of thought can constantly change association from one to another, all determined by the innate desire within the consciousness of each individual to experience and create.

There appears to be a mysterious attraction in the creativity of people who relate to one another from a group with a specific purpose. They can put an expression on their faces in regard to their art or whatever it is they participate in together, and another instinctively knows exactly what they mean. It is perhaps that they are of a certain family of thought. *We must remember, however, that free will always applies in every situation.* This means no one is restricted to any one "family of thought"; anyone can merge with many families for the joy and the creative experience.

Someone who may be of a "family" of thought who is not expressing outwardly in it, nevertheless, may also sense a connection with it. That individual may go to a gallery to view a piece of art and weep, laugh or feel anger at what he or she has seen. They have responded emotionally from someplace within, which may so far not have been within their awareness, and yet the person responds to what he or she has seen. This person thus, through resonance, appreciates and benefits from the expression of this artistic "family" of consciousness. This individual may be living and expressing in a different "family of thought" such as in a corporate or literate or scholarly environment. He or she can still appreciate the art, however, and so purchases and takes it home to thereby experience a "part" of self, which, through consciousness, originates from other human beings expressing differently and uniquely in their own lives. This experience helps the individual to resonate to a feeling or emotion that is intangible, yet it communicates to him or her that he or she is not alone; it is but one of many indications that there is more to be explored in this mystery called life. . . .

It may be that individuals would choose never to explore the meaning of such an experience; yet, when they purchased the painting and took it home, they would now have something to facilitate an emotion, and in that emotion lies more knowledge of themselves and perhaps a bit more than they have yet explored in their everyday life-existence. Life is full of these intriguing events. They are tools and reminders of inroads to self, and in these there lies a greater awareness of the relationship with the Source . . . of all that is.

This concept of "families of thought" is but a hint of our interconnectedness and *is certainly not to be limited by this or any other scenario used to examine our unlimited and perhaps uncharted choices . . .* which seemingly expand and grow as we gain more expanded awareness.

# Idols, Celebrities and Prodigies

THE PRECEDING EXPERIENCES could possibly help explain, in further exploration, how people who believe in reincarnation and who may strongly respond or identify with music, architecture or literature, assume they were in fact the noted person who created a particular work of art in a "previous" life they have lived. Understanding interconscious connectedness helps explain how so many people could feel that they could all be that one famous person. Perhaps, instead, they recognized, through some felt sense of familiarity, that they have participated in a "family of thought" or specialized consciousness. They subtly recognize this through their response to a work or other endeavors which made another famous. The initial response is therefore valid, as is any kind of felt response, as a signal or indicator that there is some significance worthy of exploration. At a deeper level we are all one with all people—famous and not so famous—and therefore it is understandable to have these kinds of feelings.

Another viewpoint (among many) is that the responding person may sense the unlimited expression of a famous one who, while in the process of creating, accessed the universal flow of energy that transcends the boundaries of the personality self. The famous one simply tapped into the God/Source, or cosmic consciousness and felt inspired, as anyone can. The observer who responds to the famous individual's creativity, simply identified therefore with that individual's experience. For instance, when an individual seated at a concert finds himself struck by the beauty of a passage, he is simply connecting with the same emotion and experience the composer had when he wrote the passage. This explains, too, why some of us relate more readily and deeply to one artist or architect: we simply relate more easily to that particular person's experience and inspiration, and those separate moments connect in a suspended time.

These famous individuals, past or present, may also represent an example of results that can come from following through with the creative spark that lies within us all. Personal idols often represent achieved dreams and potentiality, and others are attracted to that magical essence they reflect. They are often stimulated by the idol's charisma. Through association with this ideal, any one may feel a sense of achievement, even though indirect. (From the idol's perspective, his or her own creative experience is often heightened by the validating energy coming from the adoration and acknowledgement of public response.)

This perspective could be one of the explanations of why various psychics have told numerous individuals in different regions that each was in fact a particular famous person in a "previous" life. The psychic may be perceiving and validating the person's projected belief. The psychic may also, through his or her perception, be interpreting from the energy field of the client a particular family of thought consciousness, and the psychic's way of interpreting this energy field is to identify this consciousness connection as an indication that the client was the famous individual.

In fact, the person receiving this psychic interpretation will often accept it, and, based upon the degree of their belief in it, begin to be more creative along the lines of that belief! Again one can see demonstrated the power of belief. It is important to remember, however, that this creative energy was always available for expression. It is always within the innate ability of each person to access Universal Consciousness, which is fully in support of human thought.

It is quite interesting to apply this viewpoint to prodigies, such as Wolfgang Mozart. Some would call prodigies "older" or "more experienced souls," meaning they brought with them into their lives advanced or accumulated knowledge. Another way to view this is that someone such as Mozart was born into a family with a musically inclined father who assisted him and his sister, thus creating a supportive field of energy in which Mozart, through his own will and intent, aligned and/or "tapped" into a frequency of consciousness where all music energy originates.[3] He went on to create additional music with this energy, and, combined with his own unique essence,

---

[3] See anecdote about Mozart in "Introduction" to this book.

eventually created an expanded, new music form known as "Mozart."

Exploring interconscious connection is a vast and intricate adventure. The result of this exploration vastly changes the way in which we will then view ourselves, life and people. It is important to begin simply to first love the Source within ourselves, that which links us to all. Loving everyone else will more easily follow.

The most important relationship in life
is the one with self

*May we say that [the] soul has been forever in a state of knowledge? And if the truth about reality is always in our soul, the soul must be immortal, and one must take courage and try to discover—that is, to recollect what one doesn't happen to know, or (more correctly) remember, at the moment.*
—Socrates in Plato's Meno

## Chapter Eight

# The Multidimensional You

*Updating / interplay of selves / dialogues with self / a man's case story / healing the past / attitudes and health / a woman's case story / innermost self / inner potentials / change and choice / the lead role in your life*

HAVE YOU EVER HAD THE EXPERIENCE OF GOING back to visit grandparents or close relatives you have not seen since childhood, and the "you" who arrives is not necessarily the "you" they remembered and therefore expected? How valid is your experience as compared to that of your relatives, and which experience and which you is real? One answer could be that both are very valid and equally real, according to each individual's perspective.

How many *you's*, or *selves* were actually there at the time, meaning all the selves that exist within the "one you"? For instance, there is the you your grandparents perceive, and then all the you's that have surfaced in your personality since your last visit. There is the little child, the adolescent, the adult, and for some the parent role; all exist within the consciousness of today's "me"—your perceived self.

At any moment in your life you may express any one or more of these aspects of yourself. Often people from your past have a fixed thought of the you they remembered, whether as an awkward or shy child, or as outspoken, rude, clumsy or withdrawn. For them, and maybe even for you, this could have been valid and real at that time. Another way to say this is, "It was real at that moment of your growth." What is perceived of you depends on what you or an observor choose to focus upon.

# Updating

LET'S ASSUME for now, you've come into contact with an old acquaintance after many years have passed. You may have matured to become sophisticated, graceful, confident, or you may be in the process of developing these characteristics as well as all the other traits that are latent within you as seeds of your potential. Although you may have changed and grown a great deal, you may find you are still held in the other's mind in a perspective from which this person last knew you, and perhaps your friend has confined you within a framework made of his or her own perception. Your friend needs to be updated, that is to say, introduced to the additional aspects of you that you have developed.

This need for updating may be as close to you as your home environment. Your daily relationships, where communication centers exclusively around the demands of familiar life activities, can easily drift into stagnant patterns. People as close to you as your mate and children may hold old judgments and assumptions about you, and you of them, resulting in hurt feelings and communication breakdowns.

In some cases mates and other relationships drift apart, and both parties have understandings and descriptions of each other quite unrecognizable to the one being described. All too often these are spoken with the clouded emotions of frustration and anger. It then becomes more difficult to see a single point, request or consideration being made.

After all, when formally introduced to new people, as we so often are, we all have the desire to be perceived *accurately*, and everyone usually makes an effort toward that end. We therefore shouldn't overlook those closest to us, who also need to be kept current about our ever-evolving and ever-increasing selves and whom we, too, must constantly see in their new dimensions. Reintroducing oneself to others in order to update them about your changes is a very useful tool for personal growth.

# Interplay of Selves

IT IS INTERESTING to notice the interplay of selves that takes place in one's life at any given time. I propose that all the many "selves" are interchangeable and can, with a minimal effort, be easily observed. All these "selves" simultaneously exist in the now as aspects of the total you, and they can surface at any time in response to the causal factors around you.

Imagine a woman sitting absorbed in thought about a creative endeavor when her child enters the room in need of assistance. The woman then immediately engages her "parent self" in order to care for the child. While doing this the phone rings. The woman in the "parent" role answers to hear the voice of her own mother. Consciously or subconsciously she then simultaneously engages her "child self" in response. During the conversation, many of the woman's childhood identities surface, including how she perceived that parent and how the parent perceived her. Let's suppose the conversation also includes dialogue in which the parent mentions a sibling. This topic then triggers still different memories and responses within the young mother, and her emotions may range from annoyance to affection, depending on the topic of conversation, as she emotionally remembers her "sibling self."

To further this illustration, let's imagine that she finishes the phone conversation with her parent, and, as she shifts her attention and emphasis to her "feminine adult self," she prepares for a quiet, romantic evening with her mate. In the suspended moment of anticipated romantic pleasure she now engages her "singular- sexual-being self," which flows into a self that will become one of a couple. I refer to these varying expressions of self as "personal aspects," and they are the many dimensions of self that lie within the intricateness of what it means to be a human being. All selves are in a sense existing simultaneously within the individual psyche.

What a remarkable juggling act we all perform as our bodies and minds accomodate us in all these varied expressions! We are quite wonderful beings and quite capable of expressing in many ways with many talents. As Shakespeare so sublimely and astutely observed:

> What a piece of work is man! How noble in reason!
> How infinite in faculties! In form and moving, how
> express and admirable! In action, how like an angel!
> In apprehension, how like a god! The beauty of the
> world! The paragon of animals!
>
> Hamlet II, ii.

# Dialogues with Self

HOW OFTEN DOES SUBTLE, inner communication take place between the many aspects of self, and how purposeful would it be to tune into this? "Inner dialogue" is a concept that is becoming more commonly used. Why is it important and what does it mean? What is its purpose?

From an inner dialogue, meaning an internal discussion beyond words with your innermost self, you can gain the knowledge of how all the "you's" are affecting your present life. By exploring all that exists as part of "self," vast insights can be gained. Consider the benefit of deliberately engaging in inner dialogue with specific purposes.

For instance, to know yourself better you can direct conversations between your own aspects of self for personal healing. Although this can fall in the category of visualization or imagery exercises, here I specifically mean entering into and engaging with deliberate purpose such conversations as those between your adult self and your child self for the healing of emotions, physical conditions and the psyche. Consciously participate and dialogue "back."

If your present life works well for you, this exercise can empower this well-being and increase your sense of maintaining it. If it's not working well for you, a deeply and important personal door can be opened to acknowledge where fallibilities lie and where improvement may need to, or can, occur.

This is where personal diaries and journals are useful, not only to gain an overview of one's life patterns and development, but also to observe the various you's that you may choose to counsel and educate into your present wisdom so they can be supportive of your present ideals.

For example, I will suggest a purposeful technique for your use. If you choose to, you may want to take a piece of paper and write on it in two columns. In one write all the things that come to mind that you know to be true about your self. Following is a sample list.

> I have a good sense of humor;
> I am tardy often;
> I sometimes am short-tempered;
> quick to forgive;
> curious;
> easily frustrated;
> hard to impress;
> shy;
> gregarious;
> withdrawn and so on.

After some consideration, list in column two all the things you want to be. For example, a withdrawn person may want to be more fun-loving, etc.

After completion of your lists, cross out those attributes or attitudes that you feel do not support you. Develop or replace in your personality something that will support your ideal. Remember, you do not need to judge what *doesn't* support you, for you may have created it in your life at a time when it did support you.

The following is a case of a man who did this very thing.

# A Case Story

IMAGINE a man who in his attitude feels a certain uncomfortableness to speak and interface in large crowds, and yet he holds within himself much unspoken that is worthy to be heard. There is a conflict within him at the prospect of such an opportunity or predicament. His advanced position in life requires him to address mass audiences and to share the wisdom he has learned. Yet he has fear and feelings of unworthiness, so he dreads taking this speaking opportunity and sharing with the people around him. He fears that he would appear a bit unworthy, and that he might embarrass himself, for he must maintain the dignity of his position. He finds himself in a bit of a quandry, for the opportunity and the advancement in his life and career rest upon this. Long does he procrastinate and risk allowing the opportunity to go by him. He is not sure what is occurring within him or why it is that he feels this uncomfortableness and this fear to go forward and speak.

Within this man, lies all that he is now and has been, including the memory of his very young manhood. At that time, as a teenager, he found himself in school where he was expected to speak in front of his class, and he was unprepared to do this. Thus he dreaded that the teacher would call upon him, which she did do. He found himself wholly embarrassed to stand in front of the others, to speak in response to the request, and he was filled with a sense of unpreparedness. He judged himself unworthy to stand and speak, and the embarrassment and the shame he felt in front of his peers, and particularly of a female for whom he had a fondness, contributed to these feelings. And when finally he did return to his seat, with much shame, he thought to himself, *"Never* will I place myself in such a position again, *ever."* Recorded belief: "This doesn't work for me, and I don't want to put myself in this sort of position." Unknown to him, that belief is still doing exactly what he told it to do: "Don't let me get in this position again."

He is now older and wiser, and he has learned much of life. He has also gained the development of his intellect in his chosen career, and is very well prepared to speak. But the fear, recorded through the message that he gave his memory, is still on duty. If the man were to take the time to be with himself and in his contemplation or meditation or quiet moment ask where this fear and dread come from he could begin to recall the classroom scene of his youth. He would then be in a position so the man of him could dialogue with the boy of him, the teenager, and could say to that aspect of himself, "I now remember that I acquired this belief from my adolesence, and I put it on duty to keep me from being in this position again. At the time, I did not realize it would be of such long duration. What I have now learned is that I am intelligent, very worthy, and I know I am prepared. I also believe that I have things to share with others who sit before me, and therefore, being prepared, I will not be caught off guard."

Thus he reasons with what he knows himself to be in the present and lifts and dissipates the old feelings and beliefs. . . . In a sense he is healing his past with his present wisdom.

# Healing the Past

NOW SOME WOULD SAY, "How can you heal the past?

You can heal it because it occurred and, as in the case of this man, was valid and real, based primarily on his perspective of it. It still resides within his psyche. Therefore, when he has gained new wisdom and understandings, he can then reason back with himself and expand his previous perspective, and the healing then takes place. Although the incident that occurred was real and valid to him, he has since grown as an individual. By exploring his emotions and where they originated, *and then updating himself,* the fragmented energy that was being used to hold him back can now be released. This energy can then merge with his present personality energy and create more "presence" and charisma to support him in his new desire to participate in speaking engagements, thereby replacing the old fear and resistance.

By being aware of the elements of what triggers different aspects of yourself, you can select and determine wise and affirmative steps to take to express the self you most desire to be. It is important to assist and allow yourself to be happy and fulfilled in all the roles and self-images you live and express.

## Attitudes and Health

SELF.... *The most important relationship in life is the one with self.* It is from your relationship with self that all others are measured.

As has been mentioned in chapter 1, what the medical field is now more and more finding is that attitudes and beliefs are reflected in the body. It is as if the body inhabits beliefs. Negative attitudes result in illness and positive attitudes result in good health, from maintaining health and wellness to creating the desired healings.

In my own life (and I have heard the same from others), when I find my mind is beginning to romance the idea of a cold or flu, I bring myself up short and ask why. I ask what I wanted it for, what would I avoid with it, what I wanted from it. I then give myself whatever I wanted (attention, flowers, quiet time, lounging in bed)—and bypass the illness! A byproduct I have gained from this is the wisdom to avoid in advance the obligations and commitments that are undesirable. Illness need no longer be my way out of what I didn't want to do in the first place. I have learned the wisdom of saying, "No, thank you. I would find more joy in not undertaking this."

This knowledge emphasizes the importance of knowing your self. Many healing techniques are surfacing throughout the world in health clinics where visualization and affirmation of positive thoughts are used. The body responds according to thoughts.

As previously discussed, thought and attitude are being recognized as electromagnetic factors that affect the human body, which itself, as is scientifically established more and more, is composed of light frequency and vibration. Many new approaches are seen as not only necessary, but also as new options to be used to address issues past and present *before* illnesses occur.

# A Woman's Case Story

IN HER younger days, a woman who was naturally overweight made an effort to maintain the image of slenderness—the only image seemingly acceptable at the time. She found herself using appetite suppressants as a tool. She dated, fell in love and married. As her life continued, her insights and life wisdoms exceeded those of the average person. These attributes and her sense of humor were very engaging. Though through it all she tried to retain her slender body image, it was not long before she recognized a pattern of the yo-yo effect of going from trim to overweight.

In my dialogues with her I found that there was also a yo-yo effect in her moods. She was unhappy, irritable and moody overall when she was trim. This was a definite change from her more content, spontaneous and gregarious self. Further exploration revealed that in her overweight condition she discovered she felt more powerful and in control. In further examining her times of slenderness, she found that she felt vulnerable, frail and uneasy. This sense of having a sexually attractive body became compounded when the attractiveness would seemingly draw to her responses she did not want, as these detracted from her sense of being in charge.

As it turned out there were two main factors influencing her behavior. A part of her wished to remain overweight in order to know for sure that those close to her liked her for herself and not for the shape of her body. A supporting part wished to avoid trimness because of an experience she had with an aunt who was instrumental in her struggle with her body image. The aunt was known for her beauty and sexual appeal. She was also much criticized for her use of her beauty to gain social status, power and achievement. The woman observed her aunt and made a promise at a very young age: "I will never be sexually appealing because beauty and sexual appeal are weaknesses and diversions from the development of intellect, friendship and business acumen." In her trim state, therefore, she experienced a feeling of hollowness and void; she felt unloved. She noticed this hollowness in her aunt, who appeared to be an unhappy person and one who was not loved for who she was as a person, and it contributed to the formulation of her belief that a sexually appealing, trim body was undesireable. She was able to let go of her desire to be slender.

As in this case, it is up to everyone to observe their own psyche and release within what no longer serves in attitude and belief.

# Innermost Self

IN ADDITION to the many aspects of self we've explored thus far, the most important yet to be discussed could well be the core self . . . the *Self* of your innermost being. It's rather an interesting paradox to explore *core-self* and *innermost being,* the terms used to apply to something very deep and yet at the same time expanded within you. The paradox is that *this* self is seemingly felt emotionally in the depth of your physical being, yet is the result of an *expanded* consciousness and its accompanying awareness. In one sense, exploring and finding self is going deep within. But in another and ultimate sense, self is all things, and when you find your inner self you then see and even feel yourself in the expandedness of all that Is. Going inward also takes you outward to all things you see.

The understanding of "self" we have prior to the point of acquiring greater awareness contains all the possessiveness and jealousy of the definitions of limited self. This was the self that once took pride in never changing: "I'm this way because it's just the way I am. My family and people in this region are this way. . . ."

This previous view of self gives way to a greater lightness and flexibility in beingness. This is where *self becomes realized as an identity through which we choose to express as spiritual beings* in human form, being eager for personal evolution: "I see change as a way to grow and fulfill the potential I know I have." "Thank you for noticing how I've changed."

There is an ancient Hindu myth that speaks about a time in the heavens when many grand Gods congregated to determine where to safely place the Divine Spark in humankind. After much lively and divine debate, it was decided that this spark should be positioned in the most appropriate place—the place where man would perhaps least suspect it, yet where, when he found it he would treasure it most—*in the core of his innermost being.* The story unfolds with humans looking everywhere on Earth for this treasure, expending great amounts of frustration and energy in their search, ultimately to arrive at the knowledge that the treasure was already within them at all times.

It is ironic that the profound and simple meaning of life and God are ultimately found in the core of our own innermost being. This realization surfaces in inner awareness when consciousness becomes more vast, and it reaches such an expansion that the borders begin to fade between the self, God and others.

This experience is felt in the depth of emotion. At this point a profound and wonderful paradox seemingly occurs, where an emotion experienced in the core, or depth of self is simultaneously followed by a vast expansion of conscious awareness. Perhaps this seems to occur because our core spiritual self and our apparently separate personality self become intertwined in a common realization and become one in the totality of understanding. I believe the "seeds of our divinity" lie within the core of our innermost being. They are nurtured with a curiosity and *desire* to *know*, and they are harvested as insight and wisdom grow. Metaphorically speaking, this core being is not unlike an invisible umbilical cord to God that feeds and nourishes our spirit as well as the heart and mind with wisdom felt beyond the words to describe them. Our core is our connection to the divine Source of inspiration and genius. Once this self is perceived by us and nurtured by a desire to develop the senses and abilities of attunement to it, it surfaces in our awareness and engulfs our spirit with a divine sense of well-being and purpose. This can often be associated with those moments—all too fleeting—when we know and feel all is "right" with our world. This peaceful place that in given moments was found within our own soul, gradually emerges to become so large a peaceful place that it can then be shared with others.

## Inner Potentials

ATTUNMENT to one's innermost being assists in drawing to the conscious mind an awareness of the potentials of the more superconscious realms. As all of these potentials surface, they can each be nurtured into ideals and goals for developing the human psyche, along with its latent abilities and talents, thereby enhancing all life choices.

Perhaps you remember as a child when you had innate desires, abilities or interests, expressions that through the expectation of others and various demands upon you, you somehow locked away within and then followed instead a different life course. These desires, unexplored or forgotten, often become the regrets of later life.

Life's external demands and responsibilities, however, eventually subside and allow time for review of life and the subtle recall of an inner voice. This is when many remember their forgotten, hidden dreams and goals of earlier days and begin to renew their lives. For some, though, this is also a time when they feel they lack the energy, strength, inclination or passion to explore and rekindle their childhood dreams. They once again dismiss these dreams of youth, and the opportunity passes them by again.

Yet, if people consistently remained open to their inner voice, they could stay more in the natural flow of creativity and intuition with a sense of clarity as to their greater purpose, instead of waiting for a near death experience, heartache or other personal crisis to trigger the review of their lives. The evidence found in many case studies indicates that there is often associated with such crisis experiences a sudden insight and clarity which is then accompanied by reemergence into life with higher enthusiasm and increased love and compassion for one's self and others. It is interesting to observe that, from the stress of these desparate moments, where people are face-to-face with losing life, when nothing else matters, when all else is momentarily blocked from the mind, many people suddenly awaken, and their perception of God becomes very clear—their unseen connection is confirmed.

There are numerous accounts in books about near death experiences and out of body experiences (OOBEs) by medical doctors and other researchers. Many of those who experience the OOBEs report that new life-purpose, meaning and destiny surface at this crucial time. They report meetings with intelligent and spiritual beings who lovingly guide them or offer advice. As with them, our decision whether to be attuned or not attuned to creative, guiding forces is always a choice we make. Destiny is a choice we are continually making . . . either out of necessity or in the luxury of choice . . . our divine heritage.

# Change and Choice

HOW OFTEN, in spite of the guidance of our wonderful five senses, have we noticed our feelings of discontent, at times subtle and at others not, and yet did not respond in accordance with them—the room we were in, the job, the relationship—always with the fear that change would not bring an improvement. Perhaps we need to acknowledge everything is as it is because we created it that way. In reviewing our lives it then becomes very obvious that there is no one outside of us, who, without our participation, is setting up our lives for us.

If you created the unsatisfying job, yet have a fear that change might not bring improvement—stretch your mind to acknowledge that whatever is dissatisfying to you is partly your own creation. You're then more empowered to create what you *do* want because you can then acknowledge that what does not serve you was not handed to you by some outside Source.

Because you are a spiritual being, nothing outside of you denies you. Therefore intentionally participate and engage in an internal dialogue with aspects of your psyche to nurture your own feelings of worthiness. Intent and focus are important elements in bringing into manifestation your ultimate dreams.

The commitment you make resonates out, and what does not serve you begins to release from you. You begin to attract what will serve, and then your personal transformation begins. This can manifest in simple ways. A phone call with a job opportunity or an allergy that ceases because of a shift in attitude or even a relationship that improves—because when you feel unworthy about yourself, it is difficult to attract mates and others who treat you any differently. Scattered throughout history and in the present day there are individuals who were born with personal disadvantages and what would seem to be obstacles and limits, but who, through absolute dedication to wanting a better life, have communicated within their being that what they were presently experiencing was finished, a completed experience, and they began to change the course of their own destiny. I choose to end this chapter with one of my most favorite quotes. As Goethe said,

> Until one is committed, there is hesitancy, the chance to draw back, always ineffectiveness. Concerning all acts of initiative and creation there is one elementary truth the ignorance of which kills countless ideas and splendid plans: that the moment one definitely commits oneself, that moment providence moves too. All sorts of things occur to help one that would never otherwise have occurred. A whole stream of events issue forth from decision, raising in one's favor all manner of unforeseen incidents and meetings and material assistance which no one could have dreamed would come their way. Whatever you can do or dream you can, begin it. Boldness has genius, power, and magic in it. Begin it now!

*I believe the happiest individuals
and the most creative
are those who live the role of co-creator
from the script of their innermost being*

*...[O]ur normal waking consciousness, rational consciousness as we call it, is but one special type of consciousness, whilst all about it, parted from it by the filmiest of screens, there lie potential forms of consciousness entirely different. We may go through life without suspecting their existence, but apply the requisite stimulus, and at a touch they are there in all their completeness. ...*
—*William James*, The Varieties of Religious Experience

## Chapter Nine

---

# Exploring Personal Frontiers

*Drugs, desires and beliefs / states of joy and anger / roads to consciousness / not against, but for / evolution in male and female relationships / wholeness: choice over need / commitment vs. enslavement / creating your preferred future by creating your preferred life / the lead role in your life.*

WHAT I WISH TO EXPLORE IS THE SUBJECT of altered states of personality as these pertain to spirituality. As such, it seems appropriate to also explore artificially induced altered states.

It is rather interesting to note that many people are easy and quick to categorize those interested in altered states of consciousness as strange, poorly adjusted or under educated and generally seeking to escape life's frustration.

---

While that may be the case in some instances, in these present times many highly educated and successful people holding responsible life positions and leading balanced, fulfilling and productive careers, are deeply interested in higher consciousness. These seekers can no longer be placed in the old categories of occultist, esoteric, off-the-wall, wierd or ungodly—categories largely defined by the ignorance, fears and prejudice of the accusers.

Some people feel that drugs can provide a shortcut to an altered state and can create a doorway to other realms. However, the question arises of whether people can deal with the other realms once entered into.

It should be pointed out that with drugs a window can be opened where the users expose themselves to a wide menagerie of experiences, whether these be frightening or sublime, helpful or detrimental.

The predisposition of an individual has everything to do with how this experience will affect them. This depends on a variety of conditions, among which are their own subconscious programming, their desired purpose, and the place—psychological or emotional—from which they enter this experience.

# States of Joy and Anger

ANGER, although a common state, is still an altered state—as is frustration, jealousy and other emotions, all of which alter your normal state.

On the other side of this coin are the altered states of happiness and joy, as in that exhilarated place we go to when we fall in love and feel invigorated and energized and become clearly different to everyone who knows us.

People have induced altered states using drugs for milleniums of time. Yet the measure for interpretation is equal to one's growth and knowingness, or to one's ability positively and correctly to evaluate one's experience. The intent and purpose of your psychic journey is of utmost importance.

Caution is needed as it is not the destination, but rather the journey that is of importance. Therefore, if the journey is artificially induced only, it may be a non-journey, or rather one that is missed because of the unfamiliar state of consciousness. As I have stated previously, one can find natural inducements to altered states in a wide variety of activities, from nature walks to meditation and prayer.

*Bliss*, a term so commonly used in association with the altered state of illumination and enlightenment, is certainly far easier to reach from a state of joy and happiness. The goal is to develop states of joy and happiness! I support the shortcut from joy to bliss, rather than from substance to bliss.

# Roads to Consciousness

MY ENTHUSIASM, deep curiosity and love for life and people are what inspire me to soar in consciousness. This is true of many others. I've experienced that when a person soars in consciousness, the brain sends out unseen tentacles or antennae upon which thoughts travel out into vaster realms of consciousness. In a sense, those who do this, experience other dimensions that are available to support and induce more heightened creativity, and this is equally addictive in a natural and postive way.

One could say that a sort of map is set up by intention and desire. This is the trigger, the catalyst for the psychic journey and spiritual quest. When one returns from this experience, he or she finds greater insights, information, knowledge and divine wisdom have been acquired with which to add to and enhance their lives.

This is far different than one who takes artificial substances for a short-cut or to escape, and who, upon return from their experience, feels depressed or frightened because some part of the experience confirmed what they might have felt preceding the experience: life is harsh; life is to be endured or avoided. *One experience contributes to enlightenment, another may lead to disenchantment and discouragement.*

# Not Against Something but for Something

IN REFERENCE to our oneness, it is for those who have experienced the enthusiasm and passion for life to refrain from condemning those who, for various reasons, have chosen the journey of substances. It is for the observer to understand and take compassion for them.

It is far more useful to endeavor and determine to participate in *re-creating society* from one that has fostered such sorrow, hurt or frustration in short from the need for the escape that alcohol, drugs, etc., offer in the lives of many. It is far more useful instead to help re-create a new belief in understanding of self at the core level and make society a place of nurturing and honoring of all its people, a society that then would support the dignity and a higher personal self-esteem of all people.

So actually the war against drugs . . . isn't! It is, rather, a war against negative attitudes that do not support life in people and people in life. It is a war against harshness, unkindness, bigotry and selfishness. This is a war to be fought with love, consideration, kindness, caring and compassion. To use the terms *war* or *battle* is in a way to draw focus and energy toward conflict and fragmentation. When you are clear what it is you are against, see what it is you want to energize and improve instead and focus upon the ideal. When you are pro-joy you are already energizing the better world we all want, and there is definitely a ripple effect.

People will always find a way to escape if needed. Let us, as a small or global community of people, take away the need to escape. The battle is not only fought out there in reform programs, but also within—in individual and personal growth, and in the rethinking, if necessary, of our personal beliefs and conduct. The ripple effect supports clearer perspectives and produces newer solutions. Deciding to live in a better world follows the determination to live a better life.

# Evolution
# in Male and Female Relationships

IT IS INTERESTING to observe in this regard how relationships have taken form and evolved in our culture. Often people draw to themselves another who will provide or fill in certain missing traits or personality features.

Women,with minimal choices offered them, were once forced to look to men to provide financial suport, a sense of identity and community status. Through enormous effort for change, women now have more choices. This adds a much needed balance to the male and female roles in many areas of the social structure and our culture.

For example, there is now far more choice for anyone who wishes to consider a potential companion or mate. It is similar for men also who, from the legacy of tradition, were encouraged to choose a mate who could support them with total dedication in their male identity or careers. This mate would be overall more dependent than independent and not given to much original thought. The dedication of this mate was to include full responsibility for meal preparation, housekeeping and child-rearing, and although this arrangement works well for many, for others this structure has proven repressive and stagnating.

The result of efforts to fit in such a structure created frustration, hardship and resentment, which stem from the limitations seemingly placed on the spirit of these couples. The love they once had begins to suffocate in such an environment.

Men and women are now more free to choose a mate based on preferred choices. This represents an evolution from our ancestors who lived in a more constricting

structure, from which they derived many of their needs—
a survival oriented consciousness. Today there is an
emerging awareness supportive of personal choice and
fulfillment. Evolution in relationships directly parallels
the evolution in an individual's personal growth through
their evolution in beliefs and attitudes. It is encouraging
to observe the evolution from survival consciousness to
choice consciousness. This results in new paradigms.

Equality and balance begin with attitude and beliefs.
How appropriate that, as humanity evolves, the balance
between and integration of the inner male and female self
can then be expressed outwardly in an individual's life. As
many evolve in their thought and beliefs and as personal
acceptance and the integration of love of self is adopted,
we all ultimately will express and live in a more integrated
world.

# Wholeness: Choice Over Need

AS WE HAVE DISCUSSED in previous chapters, many people
are now seeking and reaching more and more a new level
of wholeness within themselves. As this wholeness
emerges, new relationships and new models or paradigms
for marriage and commitment emerge to replace the previous structure of dysfunctional families, relationships
and collapsing marriages. Many relationships and many
marriages have often been based either entirely on sexual

attraction or even feelings of inadequacy where, out of a perceived lack, one seeks another to provide a trait he or she lacks in order to feel complete or whole.

I do believe people can indeed in a sense be mates, as in kindred spirits or souls, or soul mates; yet, I feel without question that this does not mean we are each only half a person separately, and only whole and complete when with one another. If that were so, we as human beings would be restricted or enslaved to a limited belief of being inept, incomplete, and not able to experience true joy, bliss, inner peace and spiritual atonement unless we are in a relationship with that "one" other. This sort of arbitrary rule does not support our already existing and natural state of oneness . . . a condition that affords us, if we choose, personal choice over need.

Selection of a companion or mate from personal choice rather than from a perceived need creates the ground for relationships to thrive. Then relationships are conducive to growth and change, which allows, supports and nurtures evolution in the individual. This pattern of allowing growth for each partner in a marriage or relationship enhances the adventure. Each partner in an evolving relationship is allowed to grow and encouraged to explore the growth of self and the other. Each may then continually introduce the other to the growing and evolving individual they are—thus satisfying the need for newness. Revitalization such as this is often missing in a relationship where change is seen as a threat, where a structure is formed that restricts change and growth. This is the kind of structure that often precedes the desire for a new partner, which is for some followed by a collapsing and dissolving partnership, marriage and family.

## Commitment vs. Enslavement

ALL TOO OFTEN the greatest fear one has when considering a commitment is the losing of one's self and/or enslavement. By enslavement I mean giving up one's freedom; yet, commitment is an enslavement only if it is given because of the expectations of others. To repeat, it is an enslavement if it is given only out of others' expectations. Genuine commitment, which stems from an emotional enthusiasm (felt emotions) can be all-encompassing and inclusive of personal freedom when it is from the love and heart given to another who has an equal desire.

## Creating Your Preferred Future by Creating Your Preferred Life

I BELIEVE, as we move into the future, more individual creativity and personal genius will emerge. As discussed in previous chapters, knowing how an individual life contributes to the collective whole of life leads each individual to become more aware of and accountable to the whole. Once you acknowledge your own power or influence in your life, as well as your responsibility for the expressed power of God within you, you can, with more exactitude, create a preferred future of your conscious choice. We may all form new core beliefs, based upon what the great saints, sages and true mystics have always hinted at.

As the future unfolds, you realize that you can create your preferred reality. Sometimes it is so much easier to watch others participate in life and ponder, "Why not me?" Or, in the case of unhappiness or illness, "Why me?" I believe it all begins and develops within the consciousness of an individual's belief. Being a spectator of life has its comforts and rewards, but it is best if this is done in preparation for your own participation in life. Armchair living is only one of the obvious choices, and can possibly lead to unfulfillment and disenchantment— furthering a cycle of inactivity. Even in their simplest form, life and self are both worth exploring.

## The Lead Role in *Your* Life

TAKING THE LEAD ROLE in your life is not unlike being the writer of a great play. The stage is life. Each individual is not only the writer, creating the scenarios of life experience, but also the casting director, drawing to self the supporting cast of others to support or not in the lead role of your individual play. Often, out of a sense of unworthiness, many will cast others as the lead in their own life play, hoping that someone else will make their play a box office success.

As you create your supporting cast, it is important as the lead player and the creator/writer, to ask yourself if you have cast players to support you in the fulfillment of your life with excellence, abundance and worth, or in lack, victimization, mediocrity or boredom. Remember, no one is wrong in this play—everyone is acting out their own role according to their own *spoken or unspoken direction.*

At the very least, treat yourself as you would a newborn babe. Be aware as you enter a room how it affects you. Does it affect you with a happy or unhappy feeling? If you had the newborn babe with you, would you remove it to where it would experience joy? *Do the same for yourself!* Do not be around people who are harsh to you. Often a newborn is highly discerning of others who come into its presence. You have this same sensitivity if you listen to yourself carefully. If anything appears to threaten your joy, growth or peace, remove yourself to where you will be nurtured. As you would do for the babe, do likewise for self.

When you are feeling your happiest, tune in to

where you are and who you are with. Find out what is conducive to your joy and what is supportive of you. Likewise, when you are uncomfortable, intimidated, tune in! Note where you are, who you are with, where the feeling is coming from and what you are creating. Make the changes necessary to recreate your happiness.

*I believe the happiest individuals and the most creative are those who live the role of co-creator from the script of their innermost being—the one that begins with, "I am, therefore I can."*

We are spiritual beings here for the
human experience

# Chapter Ten

# Custodians of Tomorrow: Creating Preferred Futures

*Charmed existence / creativity and you / the conscious-ness of genius / from desire to reality / the chameleon-like nature of God / on creating our preferred future*

KNOWING THAT WE HAVE *always* participated in creating our own realities leads to embracing the full responsibility that we are indeed custodians of tomorrow.

Today we foster a greater consciousness within our race, from the tools of evolved and expanded reasoning, which increases our ability to create the preferred future heretofore seen only in dreams and desires of peace . . . *the future in need only of the wisdom to create it.*

# Charmed Existence

THE STUDENT ASKED THE MASTER, "What did you do before you became enlightened?" The master replied, "I chopped wood and carried water." The student then asked, "What do you do now that you are enlightened?" And the master replied, "Chop wood and carry water!"

This is an oft-quoted anecdote from the tradition of Zen Buddhism. It points to the simple fact that we can make our daily life an enlightening experience. Each action, every word we speak is a spiritual or sacred experience. This very simple and profound story demonstrates the importance of attitude. Rather than thinking of ourselves as only mere human beings here in life struggling to attain a spiritual experience, it is instead that we are already spiritual beings, simply by means of our connection to our Source. Therefore, we are spiritual beings here for the human experience. . . . As we awaken to this, increasing ease, lightness, magic and joy surface in our experience of life.

This is very delightfully expressed by Jane Roberts in her whimsical piece "The Charmed Life":[1]

Each life is charmed . . . , yours, and everyone else's, and you must never forget it. The instant you're born,

---

[1]See *The Further Education of Oversoul Seven*, by Jane Roberts (Prentice-Hall, 1979).

you're charmed, because life itself is a charm. Each being is charmed into existence in whatever reality it finds itself, and given everything it needs to operate in the environment. Your body is charmed, too: It's a magic part of everything else; springing up from all the things you see about you. . . .

. . . [Y]our life *is* charmed. And there is a secret, a very simple one. Really, it's not a secret. But you have to remember that your life is charmed. People who forget can't use their magic nearly as well as they did before, and they have a tendency to get angry at those who can. So, often, they pretend that no magic exists at all. Then they evolve great philosophies to prove it, which is itself magical, of course. But they can't see that, because they're so convinced that magic doesn't exist. . . .

. . . [A] characteristic of magic is that it automatically turns into whatever you want it to be. You create your own reality with it, so whatever maps you make are real. And if you forget what magic is, then you're liable to think that your map is the only real one, and all others are false. You get in a terrible bind, fighting over which way is right, which road or map, while all the time magic is what makes the maps. And a great variety of maps can appear in the twinkling of an eye!

Particularly when you grow up, many people will tell you that there is no magic. If you believe them, then you'll forget too, and you'll act as if you aren't charmed and bring unmagic into your life . . . which is magic too, you see, but magic that doesn't know itself. Then you'll create things that go with unmagic, like sorrow or sickness, and you'll have to deal with them at that level until you remember that your life is charmed again.

So in the meantime you'll feel nasty and unloved and angry, way beyond what is natural, and have to worry about sad or fearful emotions and what to do with them, when magically, you'd know: They'd just come and go exuberantly like summer storms. But anger and hate and sorrow are all magic too, and left alone, they'd lead you back to the knowledge that your life is charmed. Because hate is love looking for itself everyplace but where love is; and love is what you feel for yourself when you know that you are where you're supposed to be in the universe, and that you're lovely just because you are, and, of course, [are] charmed.

# Creativity and You

ADDITIONAL INSIGHTS can be gained about creativity, one of which is very applicable to anyone who has ever experienced a restless night's sleep—a night where it seems your mind will never cease chattering. This includes the realm of those experiences such as the brilliant idea or insight that comes in the middle of the night—the kind a part of you knows is profound, but which you forget, or with a half-memory can only vaguely recall upon awakening in the morning.

Let's look at some of the dynamics of this common middle-of-the-night occurrence. First it is useful to note that consciousness is not confinable. If, for example you have had a creative, stimulating or even a mentally taxing day, you may feel a need or have a desire for some solutions, creative answers, insights and general assistance regarding your daily projects and life. It is in fact this very need or desire of yours that *sends* out the thought frequency which in turn brings or draws answers and creative insights to you. Having already discussed in previous chapters the mechanics of *sending* thoughts, let's further explore this one particular way of *receiving* them. What is so often misperceived as just a restless night's sleep can be a quiet time for receptivity.

Creativity and consciousness do not necessarily recognize time as we do. Therefore, in the moments of sleep or even pre-sleep, your active self and conscious mind become quiet and thus more receptive for the assistance and solutions you desired earlier.

Consciousness is energy, whether of the creative, healing or intellectual nature and it is therefore unrestricted by fatigue. As long as it is needed and assisted, it will and does respond to your desire. I am sure this is a partial explanation for much of the inspiration that many of the great thinkers, artists, composers and statesmen have attempted to describe and share of their personal encounters with that "something" that seemed to trigger their excellence, which itself has then gone on to offer its own inspiration and stand the test of time.

Many creative people have hypothesized that this late night quiet time is the most conducive for their talents, higher consciousness and creativity. I have found that keeping a tablet and pencil on my night table affords me the ability of capturing those golden moments without disturbing my comfort and the important drowsy, altered state so conducive to creativity of this kind. Others prefer a small tape recorder. Either way it is important to sustain these moments in any way that serves you. I have also found that by writing or recording these inspirations I was tapping into the Source (just as one would answer a ringing phone); in this way I feel you enhance the line of creative consciousness, and in a sense free up more space, metaphorically speaking, for this creative flow. This flow is further assisted and more easily sustained, as well, because you do not block it with resitance out of a concern for your lack of sleep.

On the contrary, I must add that you may find the sleep you enter into following such an experience is far more restful and peaceful. Ask yourself why you are awake ... *and listen!* There may be answers you want that have come to you during this time.

# The Consciousness of Genius

THERE WAS A TIME when it was believed that in order to be a genius one must be born one, for genius was seen as being connected to one's brain and heredity. With the view that consciousness and the mind transcend the brain, it is simple to see that thought and intelligence are not merely a function of the brain. Genius, therefore, has many contributing factors in its acquisition, and is not solely contributed to, or confined by, genetics.

# From Desire to Reality

IT IS THE BEST OF TIMES...it's also rapidly changing times, a rapidly changing world—for the better! A new decade is emerging with more promise and more enthusiasm for freedom and peace, with more awareness toward the support— not just for the few but for the collective whole of all creation . . . contributing to a healthier life and a healthier earth. As Asta Bowen said so well:

> For the first time in most of our memories, peace on earth is not just a greeting card sentiment, but an actual possibility. . . . The world, we find to our astonishment, is not hopeless after all. Rigid polarities can dissolve; radical change can be accomplished without firing a shot; repression is not as enduring as the passion for freedom.[1]

---

[1] From an article in *The Seattle Post-Intelligencer*, 1989.

# The Chameleon-like Nature of God

I MARVEL at the times of our ancestors, of many generations past, our father's father and our mother's mother who, on reflection, seemed to have lived in another world. It was a different and a bigger world then. We as a race of people were very separated by all of our various regions, and all our distinct cultures. This separation was further kept intact with the strong yet invisible walls from our accumulated beliefs, carrying over between the villages, towns and cities, walls between the people and their respective governments. We even fought and killed over all the many differences which existed and, of course, *appeared* very real, including our separate beliefs in God.

Many different spiritual and religious myths sprang out of that time span, yet time passed, and people evolved and moved forward. It is as if we were all indulged in our separate gods. Now, today, it is as though we live in a much smaller and very different world than before. We have even travelled to each other's regions and homes. We've travelled and come to know the mountain peoples, and the mountain peoples have travelled down the valley to learn more about the village peoples. We've crossed the waters to other lands and other peoples. We've looked over fences and climbed walls to explore each other's lands, cultures, and their various concepts. We have woven our knowledge into each other's lives: we've shared our cuisines, arts, handicrafts, talents, and we've intermarried and learned more of each other's myths and religions. Furthering our understandings, we've become closer, we've come to think and learn of the world as a global village. At one point in time, we were further removed from acts of inhumaneness in other parts of the world. It was somewhat, though certainly not always, easier to endure. Now, because of technology, you can see in a moment what takes place in another part of the world, and it immediately impacts us, and we respond to initiate needed change, the benefits of which far exceed those of just commerce, trade, cultural enhancement and global economy. Through a closer look and closer living, it has also afforded us to see some of ourselves in each other. . . .

So, the world has evolved; the world has gotten smaller. Some people might argue for the benefit of keeping all the separateness the way that it used to be. I would disagree.  I believe that the way the world has evolved is the way that it was supposed to because through the commoness we've seen in ourselves we are gaining a respect for each other and our differences. Thus we're not as easily brought to war.

This evolved consciousness also gives way to a greater awareness not only of our human commonality, but also of our commonality and gained respect for nature and animals.

And now we stand at the threshold of an emerging understanding and realization that through the life Source or God, we are all one! And I for one, marvel at the seeming total indulgence we have been given by the incredible Isness that we call God. I marvel at and appreciate so much the chameleon-like quality of God. It is as if this God is an adoring, incredible essence accomodating our various ideologies as set into practice by our equally variable beliefs. This God totally allows. We can make It whatever we want—Black, Red or White—and we are always indulged; even if we believe in the non-existence of God, we are still indulged.

Ever since man began to conceptualize God and fit the idea of the divine into various beliefs, man's view of God has been evolving.

Now, finally, as science and spirit come together, we are seen as more than flesh and blood, and this God is now perceived also as more than any one fixed image. This is much like seeing God as chameleon-like, changing color to fit the environment, changing with the growing perception of the perceiver. Whereas the Anglo-Saxon would see God as Anglo-Saxon and the Black as Black and the Oriental as Oriental—man creating God in his own image—now God may be seen as all these and more, not to be confined within any one belief: not physical only, and not metaphysical only. God expresses in and as all things.

*Today's emerging consciousness is actually the reemergence of a core wisdom that is in everyone of us . . . it is respectful* of all that is individually unique, but it speaks to the common nature, the oneness of us all, our Divine Spark, that is in support of us and at the same time respectful and honoring of all of us, individually and uniquely expressing. From this awareness comes the final emergence of a deep understanding that is necessary for, and gives birth to a world of unity . . . a world of peaceful people . . . manifesting as an entire world of peace.

# On Creating Our Preferred Future

THIS WHOLE BOOK has been aimed toward creating a preferred future, one of heaven upon earth. I would like to end with a jewel from Edmond S. Bordeaux:

> MAN . . . the CREATOR . . . Mystery of mysteries . . . the Hand of the Creator on the forehead of Man . . . urging him to continue the work of Creation . . . Man, the chosen . . . yet he must choose . . . his talents, his abilities, his potential . . . whether they remain dreams or become realities . . . all depends on Man . . . the glorious, awesome, impossible, inevitable task of continuing the work of Creation on the planet called Earth. . . . "[2]

[2]*The Essene Book of Asha* (Academy Books, San Diego, CA, 1976)

*It will be hereafter proved, I know not when or where, that the human soul stands even in this life in indissoluble connection with all immaterial natures in the spirit world, that it reciprocally acts upon these and receives impressions from them.* —*Immanuel Kant*, Traume eines Geistersehers

# Epilogue

I WAS TEMPTED at one time to present this book totally as my story and leave the origin of its inspiration anonymous, both to avoid any possible criticism from others and to allow it to be more in the mainstream and accepted by many more people. As I felt myself struggling toward the completion of the book, I contemplated long and hard for I knew that while this message is obviously important, my role in its delivery does not exceed the possible similar role of every human being.

Instead of exploiting the mystery of this personal experience, I wish to stress my understanding that the role I have played could as well have been played by anyone. Indeed, as expressed in the *Introduction*, this same role has been played by many in history. Nevertheless, there is more that I choose to add here. While anyone *could* receive and pass on the message in this book, not everyone is interested or disposed to do so! It has been my lifelong enthusiasm for life, my interest in spiritual growth and gaining wisdom, my passion for God and the love of God, that most uniquely prepared me to be receptive of and then share this message—as well as to contribute by my own life experience and personally gained wisdom to the message itself in this book.

When people want to inquire as to the identity or origin—in addition to my own contribution—of the wisdom that spoke to me, I share what it once said to me, "You can call me the you of God, the I of God, the you of you, or simply an aspect of the consciousness of all people they have yet to meet within themselves—Divine Isness."

I will further share with you what was said to me in response to my question when I first perceived the Divine voice of wisdom as the voice that speaks the golden thread that weaves throughout the tapestry of this book. I asked "Who are you?" And the first reply was, "It is not so important to know that which I am, other than that I be, as you would understand it, a messenger of God; it is of far greater importance that you know that which *you* are, and the knowledge in which all of humanity may unite."

Because of this sacred and sublime experience, my personal gain has been immeasurable. This experience has proved to humble me, empower me, as well as expand my perception of myself to include all the selves I see in everyone else. It is easier for me now not to judge, easier to allow, to love, to understand, *easier to reason than to react.*

This experience has not happened to me alone, but also to the race to which I belong and by which I feel exalted—the human race. I do not feel exalted just by the Divine voice alone, but more so by standing in and being a member of a race that is the receiver and precipitator of such a message!

A question that could be posed in the context of this sort of experience is how centered or self-integrated can I be if I'm interested in exploring such uncommon realms. I know myself to be centered and grounded as a human being, and I have reasoned this message through and have experienced it in my heart. I have held it in my being and looked through it at the world around me to see if it withstands close scrutiny . . . it does.

I think I am, as some might say, an unusual human being, but I believe this same "unusualness" is surfacing in many others and actually exists in *all* human beings and will be increasingly seen in them as the future unfolds.

I try—and choose—not to categorize myself in any mold.  I believe that God is all things and all beings; It is a frequency, and as such, it isn't that I alone have drawn a voice of God to me—we all do at some level. Everyone is facilitating this at some level of awareness. I am discussing *attunment* to this frequency through one's attitude.

I have found myself to have come full circle. I have recognized the little girl child I once was who so deeply loved life, God and Jesus and stories that would try to help me understand who and where he was so as to be closer. I recall the struggles of identity in adolescence, young motherhood, the hustle and bustle of career and life work and how they distracted me from this childhood desire. When the Divine voice spoke to me, it brought me back full circle. I began to realize what I didn't know at the time. I now have the strength to see that it was my somewhat innocent and deep desire to know God, to know the meaning of life, and the acquisition of happiness which opened a part of me that the Divine wisdom responded to and filled.

I think the same thing happens to varying degrees in all areas of life: in the most sophisticated of laboratories or halls of higher learning, in the intricateness of a symphony orchestra, in the simplicity of gardening and in the laughter of a child in joy.

I certainly know that I am not unique in this matter. I have come to learn of others, like Albert Einstein who endeavored to find the unobvious through being in an altered state of consciousness, or Thomas Edison who would purposefully nap so he might awaken with clarity about his tasks, or the many poets and writers who report they accessed their inspiration from a deeper and expanded realm of consciousness.

It's possible to ask—and some have asked—why this has come to me and not instead to the pope or president. If some people see visions, and hear sacred wisdom, why doesn't the pope or president experience them instead— or also?  I think it is best to ask the pope or the president those questions. After all, who is to say they have *not?* They personally or society itself may not create a place for such in their lives. I simply know what I know and what did occur to me.

Let's imagine a case of a modern day Saul. That is, what if there were an accountant on his way to the IRS office in New York who heard the voice of God and then decided not to go to work? He became inspired to totally change his perspective, his life and his name from Saul to Paul. Inspiration can happen to many in various ways.

I am aware that the easiest or safest thing for me to have done with my profound experience would have been to do nothing. I have been the recipient of knowledge that has come from many in many ways. Some might have chosen to simply analyze and philosophize about all the knowledge that had come and then keep it in that inner safety zone. If the knowledge, wisdom and inspiration I have experienced positively affects and assists even one more person's life, then it is worth it. I have, therefore chosen to share mine.

To complete my thoughts about my experience and this book I wish again to quote Emerson :

> That well known voice speaks in all languages, governs all men, and none ever caught a glimpse of its form. If the man will exactly obey it, it will adopt him, so that he shall not any longer separate it from himself in his thoughts; he shall seem to be it, he shall be it. If he listens with insatiable ears, richer and greater wisdom is taught him. . . . His health and greatness in his being is the channel through which heaven flows to earth.[1]

Do you ever experience moments in your life while busily doing an act, reading, conversing, etc., and you have an elusive feeling that you're preparing yourself toward something you're going to do. I have long felt that sense . . . and finally, during the preparation of this book, I've experienced the other side of that feeling. I knew, while working on this book, that it was one of the "somethings" I'd felt I was preparing myself to do. . . .

I wish for everyone the experience of *their* "something."

---

[1] *On God and Man*  (Peter Pauper Press, 1961)

# CHAPTER HEADING QUOTATION SOURCES

*Preface:* Albert Einstein, from *The Human Side*, edited by Helen Dukas and Banesh Hoffman (Princeton University Press, 1981).

*Introduction:* Ralph Waldo Emerson, from *On God and Man* Collected Writings (Peter Pauper Press, 1961).

*Chapter 1:* Epictetus, from *The Golden Sayings of Epictetus*, Hastings Crossley, tr. (P.F. Collier & Son, 1968).

*Chapter 2:* Francis Thompson, from *The Mistress of Vision.*

*Chapter 3:* Meister Eckhart from Matthew Fox's *Breakthrough: Meister Eckhart's Creation Spirituality in New Translation* (Doubleday, 1980).

*Chapter 4:* Shankara from Shankara's Commentary on *The Vedanta Sutras of Badarayana*, George Tibaut, tr. in Ken Wilber's *Spectrum of Consciousness* (Theosophical Publishing House, 1977).

*Chapter 5:* New Testament, Gospel of John, 10:34

*Chapter 6:* Erwin Schroedinger, from *My View of the World* (Cambridge University Press, 1964).

*Chapter 7:* Fritjof Capra, from *The Tao of Physics* (Shambhala, 1975).

*Chapter 8:* Socrates, from Plato's *Meno*, W.K. Guthrie, tr., *Protagoras and Meno* (Penguin, 1957).

*Chapter 9:* William James, from *The Varieties of Religious Experience* (University Books, 1936).

*Chapter 10:* Pierre Teilhard de Chardin, from *Building the Earth* (Dimension Books, 1965).

# Limited Editions

Exclusive Signature Edition of *Beyond Common Thought*, Handsomely bound, hardcover, exquisitely gold embossed and elegantly designed. These Collectors' Limited Editions include a sealed certificate with your name and number of your volume (1,000 only), for $29.95, plus tax plus $3.50 shipping and handling. Available through Windsor House Publishers.

# Companion Book of Quotes

A smaller size ideal gift book of "nugget" quotes from *Beyond Common Thought*, will be available soon from Windsor House Publishers.

# Author Availability

Jacqueline T. Snyder is available for workshops, private and group counseling presentations, lectures and seminars.

# Tapes/Radio Interviews/Lectures/Mailing List

If you would like to be on a mailing list for further publications, tapes or presentation announcements in your area or to contact the author:

**Windsor House Publishers, 1420 NW Gilman Blvd., Suite 2152 Issaquah, Washington 98027, (206) 432-5412 or Nashville, Tennessee (615) 292-5943**

Please send me the limited edition of *Beyond Common Thought*. I enclose my check for:  Qty @ $29.95 each                                            $________________
        Shipping @ $3.50 per book,                                  $________________
        Addit'l copies, $1/book to same address     $________________
        Washington Residents .081 Sales tax           $________________
        Total enclosed                                               $________________
For additional softcover copies of *Beyond Common Thought* @ $13.95 each (for multiple orders for study groups, 25% disccount/ 5 copies or more)
        Qty @ $13.95                                                $________________
        Shipping $2.50 for 1 -5 books                           $________________
        (Orders of 30 or more, shipping free)
        Washington Residents .081 Sales tax           $________________
        Total Enclosed                                              $________________

Please put my name on your mailing list for further announcements:
Name________________________________________________
Address________________________________________________
City________________________State____________Zip__________